WORSHIP

ALSO BY JEANELLE FRONTIN:

Fiction (YA Fantasy):

The YaraStar Trilogy:

The Unmarked Girl
The Eld Queen
The Melded Truth

Short Story (Magical Realism):

Where She Calls Home

AND SHE CALLED IT WORSHIP

JEANELLE FRONTIN

Mark Made Group Ltd.

And She Called It Worship

 For information, email Mark Made Group Ltd. based in Trinidad, W.I.
www.markmadegroup.com

Book Cover & Photography by Mark Made Group Ltd.
Author photograph by Mark Made Group Ltd.

Publication Data
Frontin, Jeanelle.
And She Called It Worship / Jeanelle Frontin.
ISBN pb: 978-976-96175-4-4
ISBN ebook: 978-976-96175-5-1
First Edition

DEDICATION

To Alyxander, my son, on the day you're meant to read this book:

My only desire is that you surrender to God's will, no matter the sacrifice or consequence. Whatever this means for you, regardless of whether it is similar or different to what it has meant for me, you have my unrelenting support. Even if no one in the world understands your "why," remember that your founding obligation is to your divine purpose. All that you seek is on the other side of such alignment.

May God's Guidance remain, above all else, the one true beacon of your becoming. My love for you is forever and unconditional — and, of course, infinite. ;)

I only want to be where I can see the rising of the sun at destiny's longitude and latitude. And every day, no matter where it takes me, I will align myself to that location. In uncertainty, and even the surest of things, this is all I need know: that I'm exactly where I'm supposed to be — the very centre of Your will.

CONTENTS

INTRODUCTION

I hadn't spent more than a decade on this planet before witnessing my first demonic possession. Something evil had inhabited the sister of a boy to whom I had taken a shine. It tortured her for years, and when desperation hit, she recoiled to the one place she knew she would find peace — the church.

I saw her body wrench in pain as inhuman voices grabbed the strings of her vocal cords. Their tone, male. Their language, offensive. Their energy, monstrous...

I saw her eyes become brilliantly white as they rolled in a never-ending motion to the inside of her head. It was as though she saw the darkness, and its eyes locked with hers in that crippling cage as it remained in control of her body.

Until it wasn't. Until the casting out, the tongues spoken, and the power wielded from the Christian God halted its reign and sent those evil creatures out with venomous hurls of vomit.

When her eyes finally came to meet us, they brightened with hope and peace as though she saw not us, but Jesus. She was free... for how long, I don't remember, but at that time, she was free.

There was no trauma to be found here, despite my young age. I always knew that evil was real, even if its definition varied between cultures and beliefs. Long before these live views of its presence, I could sense it in dreams and in places, and even in people. And I respected the very existence of this darkness enough to war against it.

Soon, it began to feel like more than just respect. This war was about purpose. There were powers in the world that stood in vague but very real duality, and also in opposition. As a teenager, I somehow knew that the greyer areas belonged to my older, wiser years. I focused instead on fighting for what I believed was the good of this world, defined mostly through the eyes of religion.

I'm now almost halfway through the average lifespan of us *homo sapiens*. That fight has evolved with every dive deeper into the blurry parts of discovering, accepting, and continually journeying in my purpose. Through it all, I haven't stopped, and never will stop fighting for the good.

In the war against evil, "good" for me is seeing human beings becoming who they are placed on this earth to be. Anything that stands in the way of this divine purpose is the enemy. *That* is evil. Perhaps the worst kind.

And everything that a human does to fulfil their divine purpose...

I call it Worship.

PART ONE

WE ARE BORN ON MOUNTAINS, BUT THEY ARE NOT OURS.

CHAPTER ONE

EMBRACING CONDITIONING

Welcome to the planet.

We all arrived in the same way. Your body was pushed or pulled out of your mother's womb, and then given some form of a silver spoon, lollipop, or perhaps, quite painfully, nothing at all. Still, you managed to be here. It meant something and, no matter how shrouded it was by circumstances, you inexplicably knew that.

"Home" was your birth mountain. It was not one you had any influence over as a squishy little thing. The wise words you spoke were mere babbles to most ears, and either way, this

mountain was not yours. It belonged to those who raised you. It was the place they happened to dwell, and you were given a residence by default.

This mountain was one you intimately got to know. As time rolled forward, you traversed many of its faces and began to draw a mental map in your exploration. It wasn't long before you knew where to find the best sustenance, and where the streams flowed gently enough for you to wade. Sometimes, you were guided by those whose responsibility was your care. Other times, you picked up tips and tricks all on your own.

There were dangerous parts of the mountain, too. You came face-to-face with vicious beasts, slippery precipices, and barren slopes. You endured periods when you camped with those you called family in those bleak areas for months or years on end. There may even have been moments when those people could not protect you from the vicious beasts you feared. You were fortunate enough, at times, to come out physically unscathed, but your soul was never that lucky. Trauma left an indelible mark, and although you may not have known it at the time, those marks defined much of you.

Still, this was your birth mountain and, at the very best and worst, these were its conditions. This mountain taught you everything you knew about life and how to survive. You discovered your strength while climbing. Eventually, you could close your eyes and run along its edges with the terrain chiselled into your mind. You found hiding places for secrets and treetops for wild dreams. You knew where the sun would hit when it rose and, through every season, you positioned your bed so that its rays wouldn't strike your eyes.

This mountain had conditioned you. And whether you knew it or not, that conditioning was the reason you not only survived, but possibly also thrived. It didn't matter if it was dripping in warmth or blood because there were lessons tailored in each mountain for its residents. You were born there for reasons that tiptoed just beyond human comprehension, and this made the lessons existential. Embracing them, and their conditioning, was the first important choice any of us made in life — for better or worse.

The Saviour I Was Taught To Need

I would be lying if I said that I didn't enjoy much of my childhood conditioning. One might argue that this could be because it was all I knew, and that wouldn't be inaccurate, but with all I know now, nothing could ever invalidate the innocent love and joy I felt in Christianity. There was a connection activated in that sacred place within me which would then reach back out to the surface in a way that could be physically witnessed.

Worship was the way I felt the true strength of this connection. Singing was my ship, and while my voice did not always feel sea-worthy, when I sang with my dad, I didn't care. Something winged was liberated within me, and I jumped on every time I sensed its presence. It was one thing to feel this freedom by myself, but quite another to be free among others. Worship had a way of melting any self-conscious insecurities I had, because there was something much greater to be gained: a chance to commune with the divine.

Why did it matter, this sacred communion? Because on that mountain, worship was the climb I made to the tippy-tops of the highest trees, from which I caught glimpses of an unimaginable life. In the mind of a child, it was the life that, quite clearly, God wanted me to live. Only worship granted me peeks at new pieces of these wild dreams, and it also let me take them back down with me. They were mine to keep in diaries and daydreams, and they were the most precious thing I owned.

The second most precious thing I owned was my

questions.

Where Did God Come From?

I don't remember the first time I thought it, but I also don't remember a time I didn't think it: where did the very notion of there being a God come from? I knew what the Bible had to say about it, and I read it cover to cover — two times over — just to be sure. But I didn't feel satisfied, and because this feeling lacked faith, I sank into guilt every time I doubted. In response, I would rev up the passion of my commitment, and then dutifully reprimand myself any time I sensed my mouth watering for more.

It didn't change the internal war. There was a battle between the very real but disparate beauty of the most precious things I owned. Questions sought to uproot trees, and I could not let that happen. I needed access to that sacred, high place of glimpses. I decided that it didn't matter where God came from; as far as I was concerned, God was both real and clearly beyond my comprehension. I didn't want to risk losing the 'sight,' and because the questions didn't seem losable, I chose a side: God's.

There was logic behind that choice. It guided most of my decisions during that period of my life. We were at war with a force much darker than anything else in this world. Satan had it out for humanity, and he targeted anyone with this connection to God because they could spread the truth into the world. Many were not living in their divine purpose. It was up to those of us who were to help them. My taste for questions paled in comparison to my rage against such evil.

The glimpses I had were a gift I felt everyone should have, because those peeks gave me every bit of strength to fight for them, and for God. There was a better life laid out for each one of us, and so many didn't know it. That broke my heart, and I made it my mission to spread the message of the gospel to anyone who would listen.

The War That Mattered

It wasn't long before I became a rather dogmatic, yet passionate, Christian. If prayer was the act of talking to God, then there was never a day that wasn't spent deeply in prayer, no matter what I was doing. I spoke to God all day, every day. I talked to everyone about Him too. You could not have a conversation with me in which I did not bring up Jesus. It was my filter over the world, and through it, sides were painted, and lines were drawn in the sand.

I was taught that the devil could use anyone who wasn't saved — really saved — and this made me hyperaware of every person around me. Imagine living in the Matrix long before the movies came out, with Mr Smith as Satan. You didn't blame the humans — they didn't know. Your only hope was to convince them to take the red pill and unplug them from deception. This would result in them having access to their divine destinies, all of the associated joy, and heaven for an afterlife. Oh, and bonus: you were also saving them from an eternity of fiery torture in the pits of hell.

Converting someone to Christ was, therefore, the ultimate act of love and the greatest gift you could give. I wanted everyone to have what I had. Suppressed questions aside, I had a peaceful inner life and a dreamy family existence. My parents loved each other in a way that was a pure delight; they still do to this day. Their beliefs were the foundation of their union, and that mutual, spiritual value system gave them a love that was beyond blessed. As a result, I grew up in a home devoid of fighting and instead filled with profound, caring discourse and unlimited spiritual direction.

They weren't perfect, my folks, but they were the closest thing to perfection I had witnessed — especially when I compared my upbringing to other families' lives around me. While this evidence was arguably circumstantial, I knew it was because they walked with God.

The price, though gladly accepted, was still quite high. We didn't listen to any music that wasn't gospel growing up, and we didn't engage in any extracurriculars that could potentially border on the wrong influence. Remember, Mr Smith — I mean, Satan — was out there inhabiting anything and anyone possible in order to divert you from your sacred path. My brother and I were entirely sheltered in our early years, but my protection — as a girl in a decrepit world — was the severe priority.

Were they overprotective? Looking back now as a daughter, I can say yes, to a point. There were many aspects of life, from my culture to my social adeptness, that felt weakened by my lack of early exposure and understanding. I did not know what most of my friends at school were chatting about, and that injected hints of loneliness — but I already saw myself as an outsider in their world because I was an insider in my Christian world. This was a part of the price, but it was both an expectation and validation of my Christian walk.

While for a lot of my life, the jury was out on how extreme I viewed their parenting, things changed when I became a parent. As a mother to a son, my Alyxander (the Great), in a world chockful of predators, I'm not so sure I would have been any different in extremity if I had had a daughter; I may have only been different in approach.

Still, at the time, these subjective extremes didn't matter as much to me because I had fully embraced my conditioning. And that was because my parents gave me a distinctive kind of freedom that no other child around me seemed to have.

Conditioning Is Important To Embrace

There was never a day in my life, from kindergarten forward, that my parents picked me up in my studies or checked on my homework. Not. A. Single. One. And to be clear, it was not because they were negligent or uncaring parents. Quite the opposite, actually — education was seen as one of the most crucial aspects of our upbringing. It was because, quite confoundingly, they did not have to do it.

As a child, I believed I accounted to God and only

God. This was not just for the choices I made between good and evil, but also the decisions I made to be the very best I could be with any task in front of me. The only way I can describe what it felt like is through a passage in the Bible that had a profound impact on me:

"*I know thy works, that thou art neither cold nor hot: I would thou wert cold or hot. So then because thou art lukewarm, and neither cold nor hot, I will spue thee out of my mouth.*" (Revelation 3:15-16, KJV)

Let me tell you: I did not want to be hurled out of the mouth of God for doing anything from a lukewarm, half-hearted place. Whatever connections my young mind made when I came home from my first day of kindergarten, this was the most significant one. Schoolwork needed to have an all-or-nothing approach, and so, without my parents ever saying a word, the first thing I did upon entering the house was to begin my studies.

What my parents had inadvertently given me were my first, invaluable principles for living, and those principles gave me wings. Having such clear boundaries and beliefs for my life evoked a high level of personal responsibility in the actualisation of my goals. It's similar to the odd freedom you find in defining the scope of a project: when you understand where it should start and end, you're able to give all manner of focused creativity to it, thus achieving the very ends of the limits you've set.

When my peers complained about the pressure from their parents to study more and play less, I often smiled to myself because there were no such instructions in my household. There were expectations, yes, but they were above the details of approach and instead, focused on the quintessential "why."

This developed a bewilderingly deep trust within my family over those early years. The true depth of this can perhaps be best described from an event that took place when I was around nine years old. It was a typical Friday afternoon being picked up after school — normal, except for the words I then spoke to my mother: "I am not going back to that school ever again." The reason? I felt that my teacher was not pushing the syllabus along fast enough, and something within me sensed that this lack of challenge would be detrimental to my approaching national examination.

I hail from the twin island Republic of Trinidad and Tobago in the Caribbean. In most of my region, at the end of primary school (which takes kids up to around eleven or twelve years old), there is a qualifying exam that assesses your readiness for and placement into secondary schooling (which can then take you up to eighteen). I was due to write that exam in a year or two, and I did not want my work compromised.

My mother did what most mothers would never do with a nine-year-old child claiming to be done with an entire institution: she listened. She didn't place a call to verify my claims, she didn't badger me into staying, and she did not, even for a flinching moment, invalidate my belief. Instead, she made a call to my godmother, who happened to be the principal of a private primary school, and I began that school the next Monday—three days later.

She trusted me because she knew I trusted God. And I trusted her for the same reason. Within these confines, even the most incredulous of choices were considered, even if not always chosen. This freedom was one we honoured and treasured, and as a child, it was a gift for which I was enormously grateful. In the embrace of God, I had nothing to prove. For that reason, it came as no surprise to any of us that the assessment test on day one at my new school showed I was behind in the national curriculum, with a significant amount of catching up to do.

The Point Of Origin

My conditioning was my point of origin. It was at this point, on my birth mountain, that the first foundation of my belief systems formed. It gave me my compass and my anchor. Together, these ensured that when I arrived on the planet, I had a sense of direction that would always be relative to this origin.

Still, the second most precious thing to me — my questions — was always present. The issue was that its source felt unaccounted for and, given all I had been taught, I often perceived it to be the snake from the Garden of Eden, tempting me to partake in the knowledge of good and evil.

Indeed, each point of origin seems laced with a counterpoint — an existential duality. My duality came in the form of these two gifts: great faith and an insatiably curious mind. Being told that there was one, and only one, way to ascend to the highest points and to spend eternity in heaven, was my point of origin. My duality was so well-contained for most of my younger years, nothing could convince me that I would ever waver in my choice.

And then, adolescence hit.

CHAPTER TWO

BATTLING CONDITIONING

One day you woke up, and everything was different. You looked out through the window, wondering if perhaps you hadn't shifted your bed enough for the sun's rays to have missed you. Nope. Not that. In fact, everything looked just the same. You thought about what you ate for dinner, or perhaps what you didn't eat. You took a walk outside and sniffed the air for any telltale signs from the environment. You greeted your parents, your guardians, and sent a passing mock glare at siblings. Still, nothing. Life seemed just the same as it did yesterday, and the day before

— except, it wasn't.

You weren't fully aware of it at the time, but it was you that had changed. Adolescence had taken hold, and with it, both the dreaded and desired characteristics of puberty. Some of these changes were physical. For girls, the first bleed and swelling chests were among the alarms that awoke the beginning of womanhood. For boys, voices plunged octaves deeper as signs of manhood grew out of once blissfully smooth and vacant skin. Life went from a slow creep to an avalanche, and waves of new emotions accompanied this entry.

The psychological changes weren't as easily seen as they were felt. It was like telling someone you had a headache. As you were the one experiencing the pain, they could only empathise and, perhaps, suffer from the snappiness that came with your reduced patience. As these changes took place, in many ways, they were having an even more significant but unseen impact.

Mornings — no, days — felt unusual, and you couldn't pinpoint precisely why. You tried to shake it off by continuing to engage in the activities you usually did. You took long walks on your birth mountain. You climbed trees just the way you used to — and faster, too! You waded in the same streams and plucked juicy fruits from familiar vines. Still, the feelings clung to you like a leech, except instead of sucking your blood, they injected something into you... something that caused dormant senses to awaken.

Yes, some of those senses were linked directly to the natural biology of sexual arousal and the accompanying self-consciousness. However, two inner senses also arose, for which all evidence admittedly remains subjective: inner sight and hearing.

Your first encounter with these senses happened when you were at the very top of the mountain's tallest tree, with your wildest dreams in mind. You unconsciously surveyed the lands surrounding the mountain, which had always been layered by thick clouds in every direction. You found peace in the fluffiness of their pristinely white curves, a never-ending sea of soft endings.

Suddenly, for the first time in your life, you witnessed a strange parting in the white far, far away. You weren't sure at first what it was, and you squinted at the mesmerising variation to your long-standing reality. It was then that this inner sight activated — although which came first can be argued— and your eyes were inexplicably able to zoom towards this massive anomaly. You beheld a form so glorious that your breath caught in your throat for fear that the form would disappear. It didn't. Instead, the more you stared, the more you could hear something impossible to perceive at such a great distance.

It was a song, undulating over the furthest winds and finding a home within your new inner ears. You barely made out the words, but when you did, your eyes widened with terror. You slid down that tree faster than light. You ran straight to your hiding place for secrets, and although they were unfathomable words, you wrote them down so you wouldn't forget:

"The world needs you to come home to your mountain. When will you come to find me?"

You Don't Know What You Don't Know... Until You Do.

I went to an Islamic girls' school for the first five out of the seven years of my secondary school education. Let's imagine this for a second: a dogmatic, passionate Christian in a school that asked everyone to say prayers to Allah at assembly every morning, and if you didn't know Arabic, you were asked to at least speak the English version of the prayer during the translation.

It may be challenging to comprehend why my parents chose to place an Islamic school as one of the four choices I could specify when writing that national examination. Still, there is a simple explanation: this school had one of the top-performing education programmes in the area that I lived in. It wasn't my first choice, but even as my second, it was still an excellent school.

It also represented my first exposure to the intense practices of another religion. I had seen variations within the Christian denominations, but this was a whole other world with a totally different God. I'd been somewhat disappointed not to pass for my first-choice school — although I did spend the final two years of my secondary education there — but that disappointment changed when I had an inspired thought: God had sent me here to save as many of them as I could so that they could experience the immense beauty of Christianity.

Are you picturing this yet? Let me add some more context: remember Satan, who potentially influenced anyone who wasn't truly saved and used them against you? Well, I felt like I was going into a battlefield of enormous warfare with him every day, and I made it a point to show that I had no problem engaging with this war until I was the last one standing.

It began every morning at assembly, where I would

fold my arms as the prayers began and belligerently stare at any superiors standing on the balcony of the first floor as they surveyed the praying students lined up in the yard below. I would not be pressured into disrespecting my beliefs, even if the English version of their prayer could easily be adapted to my God. So instead, in actuality, I chose to disrespect theirs.

As an eleven-year-old child on a mission, this wasn't obvious at the time. It also hadn't been an instruction from my parents for how I should deal with this dilemma, as their advice in this area generally redirected me to have conversations with God as to what I should or shouldn't do. But, when I WWJD-ed [What-Would-Jesus-Do] the situation, I felt like Jesus was the Guy who flipped over tables in the temple for His beliefs, and that I would fall short if I showed any less passion (destruction of property aside).

I soon began associating the language of Arabic with the religion of Islam, as though they were the same. For every *As-salamu alaykum*, I mentally cast the devil out of the greeting, not understanding that I was being blessed with peace each time those words were uttered. This stereotype is pervasive in a world filled with narrow-minded or ignorant humans (as I was). For the sake of anyone reading this, let me be clear: not all Arabs are Muslims, not all Muslims are Arab, and there are around twenty-five Arabic-speaking countries in the world. It is also a beauty of a language that I would love to learn one day.

But I digress.

In my first year there (called Form One), Islamic religious studies were a part of the curriculum — it was, after all, an Islamic school. It surprised me to see how deeply principled their religion was, and how many similarities to Christianity existed. What shook me even more was witnessing the absolute commitment of their practices, especially in their prayers. While the majority of their five daily prayers would have likely taken place outside of the school system, the midday prayer (after the sun passed its highest point) took place in the adjoining mosque while students were at school.

To be deemed "cleansed" enough to engage in these prayers, the Muslim girls would perform Wuḍūʾ (Wudhu) in the restrooms, and it needed to be uninterrupted, or they would have to begin again. It completely confounded me, so it didn't take long to explode with questions to a classmate as to what I had witnessed. She explained, quite simply, that this ritual of almost rhythmic washing was to prepare for prayers by ensuring they were rid of all physical impurities. Ritual purity was a crucial part of their practices, and many rules governed their hygiene.

I was as much in awe as I was confused. On the one hand, Jesus didn't require such legalistic, hygienic practices to have a conversation (prayer) — the days of the Old Testament had long passed. You could come as you were, and that would always be good enough. On the other hand, over time, my duality arose, with three questions that I spent all of those school days pushing away with increasing force:

1. How could anyone who chose to live such an immeasurably dedicated life to their God, on levels I could never comprehend, be condemned by my God to an eternity in hell?
2. Was my God, my unconditionally loving God, the kind of God who would not see the heart of these devoted Muslims, even if they believed they had found the truth in a different God?
3. What if, dare I even ask it, those two Gods were one and the same?

Had the devil sneaked in through all of this exposure and planted enough doubt to germinate? Perhaps. The jury on this one will likely be out until the afterlife. It didn't change this harrowing fact: I felt like Peter, who denied Christ three times, but only when I renounced my three questions. Somewhere in the great distance, the rooster's crowing began.

You Can't Unknow What You Know

I was always a confident child, and a large part of this confidence was built upon my curiosity. While I did my best to abstain from anything outside the scope of my beliefs, any questions deemed acceptable deserved investigation and answers. There were only a few fields of studies that enforced this thinking above all others, and as a result, without comparison, science and mathematics became my favoured pursuits.

I adored the scientific method. I believed in finding any possible way to disprove any hypothesis I could come up with, as being wrong meant getting closer to the truth. I accepted that I could not apply this methodology to proving God's existence, but I also took solace in humanity's vast inability to disprove Him categorically. I viewed God in the way I viewed alien life — it was real, but we didn't yet have access to the scientific or technological advancements that were necessary to prove it.

Either way, there was something enchanting about what could be found just beyond the veil of humanity's reach. Each year, humans found a way to push this veil further back and reveal more of the unknown to the world. This filled me with an exhilaration that focused my subject choices with a view to one day submerge myself in the world of research.

Sticking to syllabi was the most formidable task for me. I wanted to know more than what was placed on my plate, so I indulged with the savagery of a starved soul on a deserted island. I didn't realise at the time that I was feeding my duality by creating mental maps with new paths of conditioning for how I should approach life. My liberty in investigation implied a necessary indulgence in the subject under the microscope, but there are many things a "good" Christian should not engage with or explore.

For most of my teenage years, I redirected the energy of these inclinations into homemade experiments. I took the plywood left over from construction works and built a treehouse in my backyard. However, this "treehouse" was a box that could only fit my little dog; yes, it became a doghouse instead. I played with my mother's chemistry set and microscope, ever determined to join chemicals that no human had joined before, thereby curing cancer — or at least, giving superpowers. I climbed every tree I could find, kept baby lizards as pocketed pets, and spoke to plants and dogs as humans. And when these were no longer enough, I joined my brother in committing my then greatest act of secret rebellion (even worse than us pretending we were on the set of Highlander with Duncan MacLeod of the Clan MacLeod — sharp instruments included): I opened my ears to non-gospel music.

As the most meaningful part of my existence, my divine way to the glimpses at the tippy-tops of the tallest trees, I was shocked to realise music did not need to sing of God to feel things. They were different things, but they were something powerful in their own way. Their lyrics stuck to me like hitchhiker weeds, tangling my heartstrings in impossible knots. Beats prodded my heart faster, then slower, and then quicker still during times my parents almost caught me.

I took Celine Dion's *Immortality* with me to the hospital during a minor operation. I wistfully scripted secrets into my diaries to Sarah Mclachlan's soothing sounds. I saw everything in life as ironic through the lens I borrowed from Alanis. And I became the most dangerous yet empowered woman on the planet when I combined my tastes of Busta Rhymes and Eve.

My duality had become a chasm. Once I had listened, I couldn't 'un-hear' this new music or 'un-feel' these divergent feelings. Suddenly, Eve and I — the first Eve — had far more in common than I'd ever thought possible.

Peeking

Becoming aware of your nakedness marks the beginning of your journey away from innocence. Ironically, this was why I fell in love with Enigma's "Return to Innocence," while personally feeling like a puzzle that desperately needed solving. Enigma's music was also a great mystery. The songs felt deeply worshipful in ways I was terrified to admit, as there had been some controversy about the mixing of sexual and religious themes since the first album MCMXC a.D. It was "Sadeness" from this album that grabbed the globe's attention — the audacity, the power, the fusion, the mesmerising pathways that opened through sound. In my world, however, it was an offensive, blasphemous, and inexcusable celebration of the controversial Marquis de Sade (a French philosopher who advocated for absolute freedom unrestrained by law, morality, or religion).

The issue? He used this philosophy to justify his numerous sex crimes and abuse of young men, women, and children.

The result? Outside of his lengthy incarceration in prisons and an insane asylum, he is also the reason why the words "sadist" and "sadism" exist today.

Michael Cretu, the Romanian-German musician-producer who headed this album, developed the idea as a new-age music project which made extensive use of Gregorian chants (in the Roman Catholic church, this is church music sung as a single vocal line in free rhythm within a restricted scale). As to what had inspired Cretu in Sadeness to connect with such a blasphemer against the Church, while infusing the music with Catholic plainchants alongside sensual French, he explained to the Los Angeles Times in 1991, "I wanted the combination of de Sade and the chants to be a paradox, to raise the question about theology and the Church."

I wouldn't have understood it at the time, but Cretu's embrace of paradoxical realities, whether he musically spoke as an observer of humanity or a partaker in its dualities, cracked open a door to an altered world. Something about this form of artistry called to me from a place beyond tradition, beyond restriction, beyond bold, clear lines. I want to believe that it was likely connected to the holistic oneness of the human experience, even to the divine. While I might have made other thematic choices if I'd been in his position, there was one thing I connected with above all else: Cretu, perhaps, denied nothing in himself during his explorations of sound.

Seeking

I had been running from myself, only to turn around and realise I'd never moved an inch. That's the lesson of the shadow, always there, always connected to us, and only reduced by shining a light directly from above. We can't ever eliminate it. At some point in life, when you can accept it to also be a part of your human experience, you will begin to understand its purpose.

It didn't happen overnight, but I do remember coming to understand that the more I hid from the other sides of me, the greater my shadow was cast. With that darker filter over my outstretched shadow form, my denial fertilised a breeding ground for lies and deception. And there was no one who I lied to and deceived more than myself. In my mind, I was unadulteratedly committed to my Christian path.

Admittedly, I also passively counted down the days until I turned eighteen. I had a theory, of sorts, that while I would do my best to not explore potentially offensive parts of me under my parents' roof, perhaps once I was outside of it, I could strip down and finally see what hid under my hood. To counter this, I hurled myself further into my religious convictions, speaking more and more to those around me about my Christian beliefs on everything from morality to sexuality to spiritual warfare.

Seeing under the hood mortified me, so speaking in torrents to everyone about Christ seemed like the perfect way to add the pressure of extreme accountability. I needed that pressure to remain focused on my choice of God and only God. I needed to fear the embarrassment of going against my proclamations, the disappointment that would capture everyone's expressions, the absolute joke it would make about my prior certainty in my stance, and above all else, I needed to believe that no one would ever again trust me when I shared my beliefs.

"Negative motivation" can work to keep us humans in line, but it capitalises on the consequences of a lack of adherence through the weaponising of fear. Thus, all it took, quite simply, was a sky-high pedestal, a fear of heights, and the certainty of death (of my credibility) after a fall for me to keep my truth in the shadows.

And it worked. Until it didn't.

Stumbling

My first real stumble happened while I was in the middle of my final two years of secondary school education at the Presbyterian institution I attended (following the Islamic one). The Cambridge subjects I wished to take at the Advanced Level were available there and having aced my Ordinary Level examinations at the Islamic school, they accepted my application.

I studied Physics, Mathematics, and Further Mathematics (along with the required General Paper) — all in line with my great love of research, which I hoped to spend my life doing. I particularly enjoyed my studies, but even more than that, I enjoyed staying home from school to study. I developed a system for learning that worked for me: a customised schedule at my pace, syllabus-based checklists, mounds of past papers for application and, of course, prayer. Added to the external lesson classes I took in the same subjects, it felt more effective than the traditional approach. My mother tended to ask me on a morning whether I was going to school versus expecting me to get dressed, especially when there were all-nighters involved.

My favourite part of these late nights was staying awake until my dad got up, which was usually around three or four o'clock in the morning. He liked to start his day with work, before going to work, along with the ritual brewing of morning coffee. Soon, that sweet smell of coffee became associated with focus and drew me into a state of productivity like nothing else. During these days, I felt closer to my parents than ever.

Yet, it was also the time I began to feel further away from them, and that coincidentally (ha) coincided with boys becoming incredibly shiny in their existence. I started dating a Christian young man who I had known since we were kids, and he was the closest thing to perfect a human could be. Ever kind, refreshingly brilliant, and extremely romantic, he represented all that was good about the world. Why, then, did the "bad" allure me?

This "bad" came in the form of what I later discovered

was a dare from one of my classmates to the guy she was dating at the time. I had been such a crusader of the Christian cause that this became a topic of discussion and, as a joke, she had bet that of all the girls she knew in the world, I was the one who would never, ever crack. This was meaningful in a variety of ways, but above all else, it showed how everyone around me could recognise the power of my commitment to Christ.

"Bad Boy," as I'll call him for this story, was not actually a bad guy. He was more of a deep and intriguing character who I had also known since I was a child. Of all the things he did to perhaps fake his swooning, he won my attention when he made me a mix tape of popular, heartbreaking love songs from the seventies and eighties that I had never heard. From Roxette's "It Must Have Been Love" to Cutting Crew's "(I Just) Died In Your Arms" to REO Speedwagon's "I Can't Fight This Feeling Anymore," my heart stepped in time to each of those theme songs away from Good Boy and into secret love with Bad Boy. It wouldn't have been much of a problem had Bad Boy taken his win of an insignificant kiss and carried back the news of his victory. He didn't. He delayed his claim and, beyond the small, feverish moments, he continued indulging in the part that likely got us both a bit stuck: our conversations.

The Bad Boy with the "bad," non-gospel music had managed to expose his mind and heart, neither of which were caged by legalistic religious beliefs. This sent my intrigue into overload. He represented so many things about the aching duality that was happening within me. When I was with him, while we sat in our neighbourhood and chatted about life, I felt freer than I had ever felt before. Bad Boy wasn't there to judge me — by this point, we were both very much in the wrong, and I believed I was as horrible as humans came. Instead, he unknowingly comforted a part of me that had been in excruciating pain due to my neglect of its very existence.

This mattered more to me than I expected. With him, I could breathe, and I didn't understand why. It was as short-lived as it was silly and youthful, at least to my adult eyes. Still, in those passionate, uninhibited moments of the childlike melding of minds, I embraced the tiniest part of a different path. While everything about how I chose to embrace it remained both selfish and sinful — just downright wrong, really — the embrace felt right because I had spoken to someone, finally, without completely censoring my soul.

The evening came when we knew we had to admit to both Good Boy and my classmate what had happened. If memory serves me correct, it was a Friday evening, and I let

Good Boy know I needed to speak with him that weekend while I brooded over what would befall me in school the following Monday. I had already violated so much of who I wanted — no, needed — to be, but I would not violate the act of coming clean. In the moments before my admission, as I watched Good Boy being the very best human he had always been, I remember wondering if this also would be my fate with God. Would the questions become the "Bad Boy" I would one day be unable to resist?

Good Boy was hurt, yet so incredibly understanding and forgiving — just like Jesus. My classmate was heartbroken, and my class was furious with me for not being the person I purported to be.

I had shamefully stumbled off my pedestal.

The Point Of First Awakening

One of the most beautiful things about Christianity is God's forgiveness. Bestowed unto you is infinite, unfettered access to grace. While I had lost a certain amount of credibility with those around me, this divine gift deeply comforted me.

What it was, unfortunately, unable to do was erase

the echoes, the shadows, of me. A few of these echoes were of conversations I had had with Bad Boy, but they were mostly the conversations I had subconsciously had with my spirit. Questions of "who are you" and "what do you believe" were more present than ever, and I longed to dive into this abyss, even if it meant drowning out the only Light I knew.

That part of me was now awake, and it did not care to be sent back into hibernation. The most I was able to do was continually divert its attention into my studies as my vast curiosity extended there (and everywhere). Its raging power consumed work like a monster, but it was never satisfied, as it longed for a more comprehensive, all-encompassing feed.

That impossible quest for omniscience distracted me even further from my Advanced Level syllabus, and soon I was neck-deep into the limited scope of quantum physics and the chaos theory available in the back of the textbook. I wondered, "If a butterfly's wings can flap and cause a hurricane on the other side of the world, then what does this mean for the many wings I've allowed to flap within me?"

What was coming? And when would it arrive? It was sure to be destructive to my childhood beliefs, and even my way of living — this much I knew — so, I rode the monster for as long as I could tame it, wielding its power over my studies to the point of receiving a national scholarship after my final exams. Then, right on cue, as I turned eighteen, the hurricanes began to form.

CHAPTER THREE

WHAT STAYS? WHAT GOES?

As you opened your eyes, you knew you'd finally accepted it: the days when you awoke with a loud yawn and a long stretch were over. Replaced by an uncontrollable groan that now left your lips every morning, you flipped over on your stomach and smashed your head down. Pulling a pillow over it, squeezing the sides against your ears, did nothing to lessen the increasing volume of that ever-present song. You cursed the day you saw that parting in the clouds. You cursed the mountain that called, and the winds that carried its song.

"When will you come to find me?"

"Never! Leave me be!" You screamed in your thoughts, but it didn't stop. It hadn't since that fated day. The song that had once been a mysterious enchantment became an instrument of torture. It had enchanted you because it was the first time anything different had ever happened on the old familiar landscape. It now tortured you because you secretly longed to find it above any other desire you'd ever had, and you didn't know why. All you knew was that it would mean leaving, and disappointing those you loved, who had already allocated an entire section of their mountain for you.

You yearned to share the song with your family. You even tried hinting at it in conversations when you asked questions about how they first came to be there. Their answers resembled a knowing that highlighted the vastness of your unknowns. How could you explain that a mystical voice had called to you over an extremely unrealistic distance, claiming that there was an entire mountain, a whole world, waiting for you to find it? Their mountain didn't seem to come from a faraway place, and their relayed certainty only served to weaken your constitution.

So, you pushed the voice away, and the more you tried, the louder it became. Your heart broke every time you heard it. Yet, when you thought of venturing out, your heart also shattered at the thought of disappointing those who had taken care of you since your appearance on the planet. They had such grand plans for you, and if you were honest, their plans had also been ones you'd had for yourself. Those versions of future realities, from them and you, were almost always in sync.

Now, you dreamt strange dreams. You saw unusual places, a long road ahead, many conquests, and perhaps many failures. You also saw triumph. You saw greatness. You saw the incredible ways you would climb up your mountain with wisdom from theirs and truth from yours — a combination that drove excitement into your soul. You saw the many ways they could be proud of you whenever (if ever) they got past the pain of what could only be seen as your betrayal.

When you finally couldn't take it anymore and decided you needed to see, to know, for yourself, you approached your loved ones with a shaking heart. You explained that you'd heard a call and that you must answer it. Their reaction was worse than you could have imagined. They were furious, citing the many layers of folly and ungratefulness built into your choice. They cautioned you of the madness, of the allure of dark things that lurk in great distances, and asked — no, instructed — you to reconsider your choice.

Infuriation flooded your being at their response. You

understood that they were concerned and even scared for you, but you were offended! Offended that they would think you hadn't thought of all these things, offended that they would see you as foolish or deceived, offended that they couldn't bring themselves to be open-minded. In reality, all you wanted was their support. You wanted them to let you know it was okay to go exploring a little, and that you'd never be judged and always be welcomed back.

And they did let you know that. Except, you perceived a hint of "we can't wait to say we told you so!" riddled into their tones. Right or wrong in your perception, your pride energised you to pack up everything immediately; you did. You only paused when you picked up your most precious material possession, a birth mountain ring, and you considered it for a moment.

Nodding, you placed it into the side pocket of your bag, because you didn't want ever to forget where you came from — even if you might never return to your momentarily "unsupportive" family again. Your ego egged you on, out of your home, down the trail, and then, as you stood above the final great descent, you looked back to see your mother's tears and your father's deep distress. You questioned the hastiness of your decision, but then the song called to you in a more gentle, nurturing way. You took one step and then another, going further and further away than you ever had before.

You saw the valley approaching, and your stomach turned. It hadn't quite occurred to you until then that you had bluffed about your knowledge of how to traverse such dense, wild, dangerous forests. You wouldn't even be able to see the direction you should walk in once you were below the treetops. The song would be your only sense, and that was assuming you would be able to hear it through the foliage.

You shook your head. It was too late to turn back now. You didn't want to look like a fool or a coward. You took your final step off the mountain and into the dark, expansive valley. Awe filled you, and eerily, every other sense disappeared. The thoughts of your birth mountain, the song across the great distance, all of it — because something else had grabbed your attention.

You saw a swift movement between trees and rocks. There was something there, someone there, but you weren't quite sure what or who it was. A form came out, faintly beguiling, with little flashes of light that contrasted with the shadowy foliage. As it reached out its hand, you felt a stir of relief; at least you were not alone.

You stretched yours out in return. Then, before you'd

even realised it, the form's hand had reached into the side pocket of your bag, grabbed your birth mountain ring, and delivered a magical blow of undulating pain straight through your chest. Then it disappeared.

You sat on the valley floor just below the mountain and wailed. Everything came back in a rush. Up the mountain, you heard your family calling out in desperate concern. Across the valley, you heard your mountain's song, as soft as a whisper. You tried to go back up your birth mountain, but the song's call grew louder. You tried walking towards the song, but your parents' voices softened. Confused by the pain and shock of your first valley experience, a sudden paralysis took hold as you faced the looming choice of your second step.

Rendered immobile, you then did the only thing you felt able to do, the one thing that could give you the space to think, to feel, to be: you numbed all the voices out.

You Never Forget Your First Love… Or Rather, Your First Heartbreak

When I was eighteen, I fell in love with the first guy to ever break my heart. I had been crushing on him for a while, and when he agreed to take me to my high school graduation (ball), I almost jumped through the roof. Of all the things I remember about that night, one experience stands out above all else.

This guy was always a bit silly — a practical joker. As we stood on the edge of the dance floor, shortly after entering the "ball," a romantic Latin pop song came on (likely sung by Enrique Iglesias). I remember wanting to dance to it with him so badly, but also not wanting to initiate such a terrifying event. My date, as though reading my mind, stepped forward to go on the dance floor, and I lurched headfirst with him, relief flooding my face with a smile… only to realise he had pulled back immediately and was still standing on the sidelines, having a great chuckle at my expense. He had tricked me while making light of a moment I thought would become deeply romantic (with us ballroom dancing to a song meant for Latin dancing).

We still did have that first dance, but the moment was lost. Two things stayed with me from this seemingly insignificant experience: firstly, the fact that, as confident as I was, I could not find it in myself to boldly initiate something I wanted, and this spoke to where I was at as a young woman; and secondly, I came face-to-face with a new reality, that two people could be in the same experience and experience opposite things. The latter part of this reality is probably the very best way to describe our short relationship.

I entered university two years after him, but we were both doing the same degree: Electrical and Computer Engineering. He was also a Christian, though not as extreme in practice as I was; this made for a difficult time for both of us. I was struggling with the question of "how far is too far" with all of those unappeased hormones, and I would oscillate between "casually making out is the limit" and "I don't think Jesus would even want us to hold hands." If you think I'm joking about that second part, I'm not: I gave him a Christian book with highlighted parts to support my theory of the sin of hand-holding. I can't begin to imagine his frustration with my fickle nature as I worked through what it meant to have a godly anchor as a young adult. Mind you, the entire time I was in this relationship, I was of the profound belief that it was magic and rainbows and that he was happy. Because, well, I was happy.

This guy wasn't great at expressing his deeper or darker thoughts. I don't think any of us were at that age. With such ups-and-downs, probably literally for him (excuse my giggle — I couldn't run from that pun, nor the grime of that/this rhyme), it didn't take him very long to want out… or more likely, *need* out. His approach was solid: knowing how meaningful academic pursuits were to me, he told me the relationship was distracting him from his studies, and he needed a break. I would never, and could never, stand in the way of anyone's climb. That would go against everything I felt within me, everything that "love" should be. I immediately agreed, and this would have been a sad but satisfactory ending had he not showed up at a hangout one week later, new girlfriend in hand.

Who To Blame?

I don't want anyone to think I am justifying his choice at the end (we are each responsible for our choices and subsequent growth), but the truth is that, after a while, I understood it. My doe-eyed, righteous view of the world, positioned smack in the middle of my extremely hidden but imploding dualities, made for an interaction I would not wish on anyone. Transitions are difficult enough for the person going through it. Add in the immaturity of youth and the lack of wisdom (which only comes from experience), and there is nothing but understanding to give.

At the moment it happened, I could not comprehend his choice, and he avoided providing any explanation for years. My thoughts ranged from me being played the entire time, to me being punished for "making out" by GOD, and even to me receiving my well-deserved karma for the horrible choices I had made with Good Boy and Bad Boy back in high school.

The larger issue, though, was that I felt like God didn't want me to have the love I wanted. I began to think back to the times when I had had little crushes in my teenage years and found a trend. Somehow, whether through a church leader, prophet, my parents, or my intercessions through prayer, anytime I liked someone, I would be ordered to remove them like a piece on my life's chessboard. And I would, each time, without fail, do precisely that. I believed it was a part of my surrender to God, an act of worship, and I took comfort in that belief. Either way, I hadn't fallen deeply [read: youthfully] in love with anyone, so the sacrifices felt doable.

This time, however, had been distinctive. This time, I was drowning in youthful love, and then God had busted into my secret board and taken away my favourite piece. No explanation. No questions asked. My feelings didn't matter.

Nothing mattered. I was a full-blown emo-teen in the middle of an upheaval.

I began to wonder: if God had really seen this mess of a heartbreak coming, why hadn't He busted in before I fell down this particular hole? Why didn't I at least get a warning, and if not through prayer, then through one of His usual messengers? Had I been abandoned? If so, who could I trust, and in what could I trust?

That night, crying in my bed after a couple of hours spent studying, through blurry eyes, I observed my textbooks lying next to me. Suddenly, they took on a comforting hue. A hardback, dependably taking care of the fragile pages inside, chockful with the kind of knowledge that had been scientifically proven… safe. Knowledge — science — was safe. I hugged those textbooks tightly that night and fell asleep with them every night thereafter until the pain eased.

Lukewarm Spews

It was the perfect storm. After battling the duality throughout my youth, a crack developed in my faith unlike any other. I began to give myself certain liberties in my thinking, allowing more questions to seep out of me, but the more that came out, the more cracks developed. These liberty-induced cracks rotated first around Christianity.

It started with the basic things — thoughts I had pondered since I was a child, but had never let fester within me for fear that they would incite waves of doubt. Less significant were questions about why I had grown up in a household in which alcohol was never consumed, yet Jesus had turned water in wine. More significant ones were my darker views of the church being considered the Bride of Christ.

In my earlier childhood years, I had made a logical deduction that at least ninety percent of marriages were destined to fail based on my subjective analysis of those around me (success being enduring happiness and growth; my parents being the only success/exception at the time). I, therefore, did not ever want to enter into risky matrimony. Still, if I were to marry someone, I had known this much: if any man ever came to me and said "be my bride, and I will love you forever and give you heaven for a life… but if you refuse to say yes, I will keep you alive while I burn and torture you forever," … my answer would be **HELL NO**.

How, then, was this okay for God to say to humans? And if this was the way God saw it, was He the kind of God I wanted to serve? What if the humans had wrongly translated the Bible or misinterpreted it in their teachings? Even writers with online access to a wealth of knowledge still make silly mistakes [raises hand]. Would I be so blind as to believe that whatever I had read was what was meant, because those translating it were somehow perfect and devoid of mistake-making capabilities?

The larger issue was this: I did not want anyone to coerce me into any belief — especially the handing over of my free will. No one should force me into making such a grave and sacred choice only because I was afraid of what would happen if I didn't. I wanted to *want* the Christian path from the very depths of my abyss. And the only way to know what I sincerely desired was to try enough things, see enough of the world, and find out what didn't resonate. Perhaps then, when I could finally take a look under the hood of my being, what crucially mattered to me would show itself.

While I had been warned away from the folly [read: wisdom] of experimentation, my favourite book in the entire Bible was (and still is) Ecclesiastes. There have always been some theoretical debates over its author, but most people assumed it to be Solomon. I rather liked the thought that these were the musings of the most acclaimed and wisest man to have ever lived.

Solomon chose to pursue all the vanities of the world in an attempt to find eternal meaning, and as these vanities failed in that quest one by one, they led him to a surety in the sacredness of a life lived for God. This may seem counter-intuitive, I'm sure, but I loved that search: even if he ended up right where he started, he wasn't the same as the man who had started. What stood out to me the most was that the path to finding the certainty and depth of life's very meaning was not straight and narrow. Ecclesiastes was my hope for the life I longed to explore: one in which I could reason with myself about what my divine purpose was, and what should and shouldn't be included. It felt like a great middle-ground for my duality, and I remember feeling a sense of peace that I had a plan.

The beginning of the next calendar year, in the new term, I finally moved on to campus, heartbreak in one hand and hope in the other. I was now a self-appointed scientist exploring the life of a creature called Jeanelle. A month or two later, I was ready to begin my first experiment: going to a campus dance. I lived in an all-girls hall, and I arranged to go and return with a group of those girls who also planned to attend. On the day of the dance, with excitement coursing through me, I got a call from my mother, whose "campus spies" had somehow told her of my intentions.

I tried to explain to her that I simply wanted to experiment and understand the fullness of life. I reminded her of Solomon's quest for finding this very meaning, and said that my decision wasn't a departure, but merely an exploration. I described my middle ground. And then, she told me the one thing that changed everything for me, the scripture verses that, as I mentioned previously, mattered to me above all others:

"*I know thy works, that thou art neither cold nor hot: I would thou wert cold or hot. So then because thou art lukewarm, and neither cold nor hot, I will spue thee out of my mouth.*" (Revelation 3:15-16, KJV)

She reminded me that God required us to be hot or cold, or else we would be spat out of His mouth. She didn't know what the impact of those words was for me, or how deeply connected I had always felt to that scripture. A reverence arose.

My response was: "You're right. And I don't want to be spewed out of God's mouth. So, I choose to be cold."

Dance Like Nobody's Watching

Attending my first party was cathartic. The only experience I had had prior to that was a brief stint at one of my best friend's sixteen-year-old birthday bash (which my mother promptly picked me up from after hearing the type of music in the background). This party was far removed from that sweet sixteen.

In my country (Trinidad and Tobago), the legal drinking age is eighteen, and everyone in attendance was at least that. Unregulated, unsupervised, unadulterated celebration bled through each person in every square foot of the small space. It was glorious!

I had never witnessed this kind of freedom and joy. I had always had a view that these "devil places" would feel dark and sinful, yet this was not remotely like that at least, not from my now "cold" standpoint. There was a strange innocence to the glee of the soca [an indigenous genre of music] and spontaneous choreography of the dancehall [from Jamaica] that made me laugh from a purely uninhibited place.

I, however, did not have a clue about how to dance or "wine," or even how to interact in these social scenarios. I was way out of my depth. Thankfully, though, I knew most of the people there, as it was a party between the halls themselves. This also meant that most of the people there knew me — the Bible-thumping me, the virginity-ring me [we'll get to this], the all-y'all-need-to-be-saved me.

There were mixed reactions. Some were pleasantly surprised. Others were even more judgmental of me than I had been of them, and rightfully so: the girl who had judged others for going to these "devil dances" was now attending one. She was attempting to move her body in what was likely a quite nerdy way. Thankfully, a guy from my class, with whom I had a constant cheeky exchange, saw me beginning to look overwhelmed. He approached. The familiar face helped. The genuine church-girl teasing helped too — I could only laugh at myself, at how naïve I had been to see this as anything worse than the fun it was.

This isn't to say that there weren't people who took it too far, whether in the drinking or the lustful approaches, but in general, the energy of the place was one of fun fellowship. It didn't remotely resemble a worship service in church, but it did feel like a diverse way to celebrate life. It reminded me of the contrast between reading the Bible and reading an incredibly insightful non-fiction book: they served two distinct purposes, but both allowed a connection that could lead to thought provocation or emotional musing, at the very least.

But there was a price to dancing like nobody was watching: people were watching. The rumours of my departure from Christianity spread like a wild, unholy fire throughout the God-fearing community. My closest Christian friends, one of whom I had converted in high school, were heartbroken by my choice to backslide so wilfully from God. They did not want to be unequally yoked with a now-sinner like me, so they distanced themselves, only connecting to try to convince me to come back to the Christian path. The loss of precious friendships with those who I shared my massive, secret dreams with felt like a stab to my core.

Even my less Bible-thumping and "unsaved" friends [with a few exceptions] began to express their distaste. I had broken free of a box I had chained for years, and while they had always been revellers, they didn't know how to function with me now being present in parties. I was the friend who had raised an eyebrow at their less-than-righteous choices, the friend around whom they never could feel entirely comfortable, and yet here I was, devoid of raised eyebrows in the very places they hadn't needed to worry about seeing me. People don't like it when you change on them, and even less so when it's extensive and unexpected. I had underestimated how much my extreme internal attempts at balance also served as a balance for others in dealing with me.

I felt lonely and abandoned when faced with the conditional love of those I believed I had loved unconditionally. I had a few crushes surrounding me, but they weren't serious enough to share the depths of my pain. I needed to talk to someone, anyone, but no one was there. Even my roommate at the time was also a Christian, who expressed her disappointment in both words and silence. Where I lived wasn't safe; nowhere was safe.

One day, I was in the electrical lab when a young man entered. I recognised him as the ex of another Christian girl I adored. She lived in my hall and was, unfortunately, among those who hadn't been pleased with my departure from Christianity. This guy and I struck up a conversation, and it seamlessly led to that topic. He claimed to face a similar battle, trying to be a good Christian, but continually finding himself thrown from the path.

Relief flooded me at being able to talk to someone about how difficult and lonely the transition had been. While I didn't share everything, I found so much peace in the exchange that it didn't strike me as unnatural for us to exchange contacts and keep in touch.

The Virginity Ring

One of my most meaningful possessions was my virginity ring. It was a gold piece with two dolphins coming to meet each other at their heads. I had chosen that symbolism as, back then, the myth that dolphins were the only animals besides humans to engage in sex for pleasure was pervasive [this is scientifically arguable for many reasons]. Still, the symbol didn't matter.

What mattered was that this was the ring I planned to give my husband (should *that* ever happen) on our wedding night — the man upon whom I would have waited to share this part of me. This wasn't something I kept private, because I wore it on my ring finger. It naturally provoked questions from those who observed it — predominantly, the campus boys.

There were two in particular who teased me religiously about this ring, ever awaiting my date with reality so they could get their laugh at my naivete. It made me even more determined to prove them wrong, and so the annoying banter waged on for months. When I departed from Christianity, their approach felt like vultures waiting for the absolute death of my innocence so they could pick at, or rather *on*, my decaying carcass.

I ignored them, as I did most people, as I felt increasingly misunderstood, while still dealing with my more private pain. It was the guy from the electrical lab who became my confidante, and it wasn't long before that connection slid down the slope of romance. It wasn't a wild love, nor a profoundly fulfilling one. It was perhaps even one of convenience — two souls with an intersecting challenge who provided comfort that was absent from others. Stolen kisses here, little musings there, and suddenly I found myself in an odd relationship that had crept up from the shadows of my unresolved issues.

This caused chaos in a way that hadn't even crossed my mind when we first connected: his ex, who lived in my hall, of whom I was very fond. It had been easy to become so caught up in my problems that I never considered the consequences of the unhealthy ways I chose to deal with them. She had already been disappointed in my backsliding, but now she was hurt. I was also new on the hall, dating the ex of an older hall-mate; this was seen as against the rules on many levels.

Just like that, the places I was no longer welcomed included not only my room, but the entire hall in which I lived. There was nothing I could do to change that, but I could stay away from it as much as was possible. I dove deeper into the escape of this guy, more and more despondent about what had become of me. I used to be a good person, a good Christian, but now I feared I was lacking even the essential ethical consistency necessary for navigating life. I had begun to reap the weeds of seeds sown in naïve innocence, and the cost was higher by the day.

The more I beat myself up, the further I allowed my physical relationship with this guy to continue. What was the point anyway? I had already failed so much as a human. But then, the fated day came when it was finally about to go too far, and I wasn't ready to lose my virginity to someone with whom I didn't want to spend the rest of my life, or even the rest of my university years.

I should digress a bit here and give a little context regarding the extent of my sexual knowledge. When I was twelve or thirteen years old, my Physical Education teacher held a class about the effect of our menstrual periods on sport participation. She explained, quite simply, that unless we were in pain, our periods should never prevent us from engaging in any type of sport whatsoever. I was a smart kid, so my hand shot up in the air in complete opposition — she had forgotten about swimming and the fact that you couldn't swim with a menstrual pad. Everyone in the class looked at me like I was a raving madwoman, and my teacher compassionately repeated her statement (maybe hoping I had had a brain slip).

My opposition raged with increased passion. I began to explain the logistics of how pads work, and that I had yet to see a swimming suit designed to prevent water from getting in there, and that if it did, that would cause a trail of blood to be diffused into the water. She eventually told me to speak to my mother about it, as she recognised I had been sheltered from the existence of tampons (or the inserting of anything into one's vagina for that matter).

Here I still was, in university, as a sheltered girl who had never understood how to insert anything anywhere. And to be honest, I wasn't quite certain what each part was for, or even what they were called. Yet, I was now lying on a bed with a guy whose intention was to stick his "something" into that very "somewhere."

Of all the things I felt, embarrassment was chief among them. Ashamed to be so ignorant, I didn't want to disappoint, but I also didn't want to give up my prized possession. He knew I was a virgin and he knew about the virginity ring, but there was a casualness to his expectation that made me feel like I was the one who had got it wrong. He wanted only to touch but not insert, he said, and I believed him because who would be cavalier about taking his so-called girlfriend's virginity? The "touch-only" didn't stay that way, and my timid opposition eventually felt so pointless, I just gave in.

When it was all over, I cried while the numbness slowly wrapped my body from my now "unsacred" spot outwards. This was how I lost one of the most precious things to me; the only thing that I had consciously retained from my past life. He seemed confused by my tears, only later explaining that he thought I had claimed to be a virgin because that's what women did (so they didn't seem sexually loose). This had been the reason for his carefree, careless, uncaring approach.

Don't get me wrong: I knew he cared for me in some sense. I knew there hadn't been malicious intent. It didn't matter anymore to me, because nothing could change it. This was something I could never get back. I took off the ring and handed it to him. Finally, the numbness reached my eyes, and the tears stopped.

A Crucial Pause

Before I continue, I want to appeal to any girl/ woman and boy/man reading this. If there is ever a point when you don't want to experience something physical (or mental or emotional), regardless of your experience or how much love is involved, be clear, be strong, and be extremely vocal.

Guys, unless a woman is joyfully shouting "YES," do not assume consent — even if her legs are wide open. Body language is not enough. A half-hearted agreement is not enough. Someone eventually giving in after whispering "no" is not enough. Ladies, it is okay not to know what you want, and to take the time to figure it out. Until you are a billion percent sure, the only answer you should **shout** is no. And if you've been through what I have, or much worse, know that you are **not** spoilt! You are precious, sacred, and constantly, divinely renewed.

At the time, I was too confused, too timid, too lonely, too stuck in despair, and eventually too numb to even disengage from the relationship after this happened. I didn't have an anchor. I felt broken and useless; I believed I had deserved my first sexual experience to be this painfully unfulfilling. While I did confront him a few years later about what had happened, I never told him how I felt when it did. I kept it sealed away inside of me. This was the darkness, the beginning of my valley journey through which I have learnt many of my life's greatest and most meaningful lessons.

The catch? I signed up to learn them all the hard way.

The Point Of No Return

I did give Christianity one last try, though. I went with my mother on a mission trip to Canada the summer after this happened. She knew I had lost my virginity (she asked; I said), but not the details. I believed then that this knowledge would have only caused further distress to an already-difficult, new reality. I also wanted my parents to believe this had been a wholly considered choice because anything else would weaken the validity of my stance — my pride wasn't prepared for such a hit.

Needless to say, my parents were extremely pained that I hadn't waited to give my virginity ring to the man God wanted me to marry (whoever he would be). I couldn't blame them. From their perspective, they saw a drastic and unexpected switch from the God-fearing daughter they were proud of to a daughter they didn't even know. I had hidden so many of my internal battles that my mask felt like the real deal (even to me, most of the time).

The mission trip was, perhaps, my mother's way to try to get me away from that new life long enough to regain some perspective. It was a kindness for which I will forever be grateful as she had gifted me with a much-needed respite from a looming, deep depression. Instead of dealing with my trauma, however, I used the journey as a way to sweep all that had happened for my first year of university straight under the rug. My lack of knowledge on how to deal with these kinds of situations, further compounded by my inability to trust or rely on those who had been close to me, didn't allow for any other option at the time. I also saw therapy as a need that only the weak possessed. I was broken, but I believed I was strong.

The voyage itself was magnificent. I played the drum kit for a fair amount of the time we were there, and I also enjoyed singing to the beautiful worship. We journeyed from one American Indian village to another, heading all the way north, until we were just a few degrees below the Arctic Circle. I witnessed events that I could only describe as divine, and there was no denying the power that dwelt within

Christianity. There had never been any denial of this for me, in fact — only the profound denial of my other sides, and an inescapable issue with the need (in Christianity) for all other beliefs to be wrong.

As much as the impact of the mission trip remained with me upon our return, the numbness had never left. Healing stood no chance in remotely accessing what was under my impenetrable rug. My shame and guilt and hate for my choices had severely broken whatever connection I felt. I did not allow myself anything beyond the cold, both for fear of being spewed out, and for my need to step away from the hot.

I wondered if I had always been a horrible person masked by my Christian beliefs. Did I not have any sense of right or wrong without a WWJD hanging on my wrist? Who would I have ended up being without the foundation I was given? I needed to know. I decided to start over and assume a life in which I had never experienced Christianity. I wanted to know what my choices would be if I chose without any influence from God. I needed to know who I was without any conditioning whatsoever. It was the point of no return.

My mother, filled with agony and having tried her very best, made one request: that I never sing for anything that wasn't for God. This shot bolts of pain through my vocal cords as, while I had decided to be cold, singing was my only way to access those divine glimpses. I closed my eyes and agreed, and like Ariel in the Little Mermaid, to explore a legged life on these shores, I gave up my voice.

PART TWO

FINDING YOUR MOUNTAIN MEANS VENTURING THROUGH VALLEYS

CHAPTER FOUR

CRACKS LEAD TO BREAKS

You would have loved to pretend that you had prepared for everything that had happened up until this point. You had envisioned the beginning of a journey filled with pride and courage, taking step after confident step through the valley to the sounds of birds and the gushing of rivers. You would have seen your mountain drawing nearer as the cool breeze greeted you with songs that made your heart light. Each stride would have lifted you higher.

Then, when you arrived almost as quickly as you'd left, the mountain itself would have bent to greet you with a strong embrace, having awaited your arrival since the day you were born. It would have shouted to all of the surrounding ranges that destiny had come, with its jubilance reaching even your birth mountain. Your family would have heard the announcement and celebrated, sending gifts and loving letters upon the wings of doves, while all the world rejoiced along with them that you had finally found your true home.

Instead, a burst of manic laughter punched through your stomach at the delirious delusion you had indulged in, and you took another weak step towards nowhere in the valley of your unbecoming. It had been countless months, maybe even years, since you left your birth mountain. You had chosen to numb yourself to the call of your family and the song of a distant destiny, so you had wandered until you lost all sense of direction and time.

The shock of the beginning had rocked your world, but it was everything that happened next… words you could barely utter and thoughts you could hardly contemplate… those were what had been too much. Too much for your sheltered soul, too much for your weathered spirit, too much for a woman who knew nothing other than how to be a naïve little girl.

Demolition Begins

There's a price to evacuating the only identity you've ever known: nature abhors a void, and in the flood to fill it, you will have no control over what's going to enter in its place.

I started my second year in university with equal parts excitement and dread. It wasn't an entirely clean slate, but I believed my internal slate to be clean. This essentially meant I was ready to examine several viewpoints and their accompanying principles to decide whether they were worthy of becoming part of my new foundation. In theory, this was quite a solid approach. In reality, my new-foundation hypothesis was flawed from the start, so the results of my experiment would never have been accurate.

A foundation isn't meant to be ripped up with a house (read: life) already built upon it. The house itself will crash if the demolition isn't properly planned and calculated to cause the least amount of unintentional destruction. Imagine me, instead, pulling up the slabs of concrete upon which load-bearing walls stood, while expecting the house not to come crashing down on me.

It felt small when I started. Deceptively small. And the truth is, it wasn't all bad. I had a new roommate from

Jamaica when I moved back to the hall after my summer away, and she was an incredible human being. Unlike the rest of the new crop of first-year students, she was a bit older and had both work experience and life experience — neither of which I had at the time. Perhaps the greatest relief I felt was that she wasn't the dogmatic Christian I used to be. Yes, she had a strong spiritual anchor, with a boatload of principles, but she also knew how to enjoy life with a guilt-free effortlessness I adored.

We became instant friends, me with my vast ignorance of the world and her with the charm of an accepting soul. She wouldn't have known it, but her openness was such a contrast to most of my other friends' attitudes that I drew deep comfort from her presence. And the best part was, her friendship came with others — the Jamaican girls who lived on the floor below ours.

Perhaps if they had been around to witness the drastic change that had happened, they wouldn't have been as open. Yet, to this day, I don't believe that to be true because of who they each were to me. They embraced their changes with an authority that was borderline intimidating for anyone who dared oppose them. Who they decided to be today was theirs to be, with lines boldly drawn; if you had a problem with it, it was better that you kept it to yourself and minded your business.

This wasn't to say they didn't seek counsel; nor were they without imperfections or failings. They just repeatedly owned them, almost with a savage awareness that to do anything else was futile. I can't speak of all Jamaicans, but these were my hall-mates and friends. Had I been more aware of the wise exposure I was getting by their example, I might have learnt how to embrace the evolutionary process of a slower build.

But, let's not forget, I was busy crashing a sledgehammer all over my foundation, engaging in disruptive, destructive revolution. I was akin to an activist who screams naked in the streets with placards that say, "CLOTHES ARE BONDAGE!" while not knowing for what or whom I was fighting. I didn't want to see the same person in the mirror, a person who had been too timid to explore her free will, so I dyed my hair with blue and whitish-grey streaks, pierced my nose, and at times donned coloured contact lenses. As for my Jamaican friends, what I subconsciously took from them instead, what the void temporarily sucked into me, was their language.

Talk Is Expensive

It all started with a vague amusement at the slang words that were indigenous to their land. Jamaica (and all Caribbean islands to my knowledge) has a native language called patois or creole. Of all the parts of it to intrigue me, their curse words stood out above all else. To my "Trini" ears, they didn't sound vulgar or insulting. Instead, their intonation charmed me.

My favourite, "*bomboclaat*," — a common expletive that could occur in situations of anger, shock, and even excitement — had the same auditory effect on me as terms like "mumbo jumbo" or "Dumbo." I'm laughing as I try to say it now with the Jamaican sharpness that could be placed into it, and I am *epically* failing, so I can't begin to imagine how terrible my attempts were back then.

Still, I felt like I had learnt a secret code that most of my counterparts didn't know. More than that, being a part of this circle with their new ways to speak and new ways to see the world gave me my first sense of belonging since I had entered university. However, there was a price to this, a subconscious one, that became the bane of my then existence.

I didn't notice it at first, and when I eventually did, there wasn't anything I seemed to be able to do to stop it. I would say "normal" words, strung together in their "normal" sentence structures, like I always had, but the looks on the faces of those hearing the words began to change. A little squinting here, a slight grimace there, and then full-blown, eye-rolling disdain: my accent had changed.

This unstoppable, annoying, embarrassing, void-flooding conditioning was only further intensified by my first "real" relationship, which happened to be with a Jamaican guy I met that year. I couldn't halt this verbal flow without remaining exceedingly conscious of every single word coming out of my mouth as they formed, moment by moment; there was no way I could stay that conscious all of the time, and this made the impression worse. It seemed like I wilfully switched in and out of it, putting on a fake accent over my voice depending on how I wanted to speak. My Jamaican friends didn't seem to mind or care, but for those from my country, it appeared disloyal and perhaps borderline unpatriotic.

I don't know who could think that anyone would deliberately sign up for this kind of humiliation from their peers, especially after the first year I'd already had, but this was exactly how it was treated — as a choice. And the truth is, had I been in their positions, on the receiving end, I might have treated it very much the same. It took me a long time to research the cause of the "wandering accent," the "chameleon effect," and "bidialectalism," especially its relationship with identity, but when I did, I was somewhat relieved to see that there were people around the world who suffered from the same.

Of all the many reasons researched and then deemed as triggers for "unintentional mirroring," a social desire to fit in was among them. This resonated for obvious reasons. Perhaps some part of me did reject aspects of where I was born and my upbringing, but it hadn't narrowed its scope to just religion; my family, friends, society, and even the local landscape were all within the blast radius. I boomeranged all the rejection I perceived, and in my desire to have people I could trust, my vocal cords seemed to acclimatise to those who showed themselves as trustworthy.

I plunged into immense shame. I wanted to sweep it under the rug of "let's pretend this isn't happening" [probably alongside a lot of the content in this book] because it is much easier to do that than to face past parts of your life that irk your very soul. However, to run or hide from any of it, I've discovered, is a dangerous curse we place on ourselves.

When I accepted that I could no longer speak freely without some essence of persecution in visual or verbal form, I did the only thing I had left to do: I owned it. Bitterly. Insecurely. Scornfully. But I owned it. I refused to be overly tortured by my self-inflicted judgements on top of everyone else's, and I refused to distance myself from the girls and guy who brought me more peace and comfort than they even knew. I chose them over those I perceived as offering conditional love. I chose them because they were a haven from the brutal world outside and inside of me.

It was a valiant choice, but it wasn't until I was approached by a local journalist to do an interview on my university experience that I understood that bravery does not eradicate mockery. While it was supposed to be a feature on another girl and me, and our views on campus life, he spent a large portion of it writing disparaging jokes about my "slight Jamaican accent," even though he had never asked a question about it in the interview.

Could I blame him? Not really — not if he wanted to write pieces that sold papers. Back then, however, I felt utterly deceived. Had he revealed his intention to do an exposé on my vulnerabilities, rather than a straight Q&A, I would have declined. I hadn't begun to process or even understand my trauma, and I wouldn't have allowed anyone else to share prejudiced takes on it without my approval.

He did get those sales, though. Some of the halls' residents, in equal brutality, bought several copies, pinning them up everywhere in celebration of my deep and misplaced shame.

Love Is Also Expensive

It was my Jamaican boyfriend who helped me through it. He was also the one who showed me that there was far more to sex than painful memories, and far more to love than what was right or wrong. Life was complicated; *we* were complicated. We both had baggage in different ways, and I was immature and inexperienced in how to deal with real relationships.

Still, I did my best. I loved in the ways I knew how, and a few times over, I miserably failed, all the while holding on to the one principled thing we seemed to share: no matter what had happened, we would be honest with each other, even if it wasn't right away. I could ask him anything, and with enough pressure, even hurtful truths would be coerced out (and vice versa). Something felt weirdly right about that. I appreciated it, and him, because it was my first time navigating a duality. The duality was this: everything doesn't need to be right for love to be right. The existence of this duality didn't lead to an ultimatum. Instead, a need for continual growth allowed us to get closer and even survive.

Despite the relationship's turbulent nature, I found myself feeling lighter and brighter inside. He was a good person, brilliant mind, ever attentive, with a passion for fashion and, of course, dancing to dancehall music. All of my Jamaican friends (hall-mates) shared that, and each new term would herald a wave of new dances, with lessons before the first party. After a while, I didn't care much for partying with anyone other than my hall-mates.

My life became two main activities: hanging around with them for a smaller part of my time, and deep-diving into my courses, assignments, and studies for the larger part, with my two girlfriends from class (sleep being optional). I was closer to one of the two girls, in particular, having known her since high school. Despite her understandable wariness of my sudden changes, alongside our small moments of turbulence, she stuck by me.

During those months, I rarely made time to visit home; my parents and I still had a strained relationship. I invested my time and focus on the work and relationships that I hoped would build my future, rather than the painful memories I had left behind.

I believe this broke my mother's heart. She would come to campus often, pursuing courses of her own, but also desiring to see me in an effort to keep the channel open. Then, of all the things to happen, my father got an opportunity for them to migrate with his job, and they chose to move to the furthest, most opposite place they could have when compared to our tropical Caribbean country: Alaska.

The countdown was on for their departure, and while some part of me was shocked by the decision, other parts were relieved that there would no longer be pressure in the form of their physical presence. I began to pull away; I didn't intend to have a final goodbye filled with grief and regrets. This countdown had the opposite effect on my mother. She wanted to see her kids as much as possible before their migration. Perhaps she hoped to leave behind a daughter who had returned to Christ. Naturally, I was not impressed; nor was I remotely open.

There was one particular instance, coming close to their departure, when she requested a visit, and I snubbed her bid. My reasons were technically valid at the time: I had a massive project due the next day, and I was going through hell with it. My boyfriend had taken such good care of me that day, and I refused to break my flow to meet with her and hear all the reasons why I should return to religion. I wanted a clean break.

My mother, perhaps stricken with fear that her in-person opportunities were diminishing, made up a far worse story in her head about why I had rejected her desire and shared this story with my father. He was terribly upset to hear it. The result was a phone call from my father, just as my boyfriend was walking me back to my hall, having completed my assignment late that night. My father gave me what I can only describe as an ultimatum, and I, in turn, gave him the best backchat I could produce after a stressfully long day. The contempt and fear on both sides led to this call ending in a complete cut-off of all financial support because of my wilful rebellion. It also felt like the potential end of our relationship.

Mind Over Matter

Fear gets a bad rap, and justifiably so — many mistakes are made under the barrel of fear's gun. My parents were likely terrified of a life in which I did not know God, but this fear drove them to try to control the uncontrollable (me). Had I allowed myself to be vulnerable enough to let them in, to let them know what I had faced, I doubt it would have ever come to this. Instead, all they experienced was their kind, respectful, and honourable daughter suddenly not caring remotely about anything they had ever taught me, or everything they had sacrificed for me to succeed.

Their circumstantially-driven choice had hinged on their greatest fears coming to life, but even as a destructive force, that fear was still crucial to have. Fear is important. Yes, it can restrict your wings, but when healthily embraced, it can also show you how to fly. It will plant seeds for future growth if we allow it to trigger a need for change. My parents eventually did precisely that — grow, and beautifully so — whilst I did something catastrophic: I pretended fear didn't exist.

I scorned the smell of fear on them, although in reality, I was only sensing it within myself. Why else would I not share the truth of my story?

I chose to mask the fears that plagued me with a false sense of courage. This resulted in some of the dumbest decisions of my life. I adopted the concept of "mind-over-matter," and it is a powerful one, but not when the "matter" really matters.

Allow me to provide some humour for a minute as

I recall my only experience of a blackout from being drunk! I had convinced myself that intoxication was a mind-over-matter issue. I decided to prove my hypothesis, and my test subject was none other than myself. I went to a club one night with a few of my hall-mates and, having hardly ever consumed alcohol before, decided to try to keep up with a well-seasoned drinker.

We each took four shots of tequila straight, and then drank six bottles of Smirnoff Ice. In the inevitable state of drunken delirium that followed, I celebrated how powerful my mind was when freed from its fears. A good friend came up behind me to dance, and as I confidently leaned back into what I thought was him, I was greeted by the cushy comfort of the club's floor.

My hall-mates hauled me to the car, and I don't remember anything else from that night besides some scattered pieces, which did scare me. To be devoid of all control over your body and mind, while inside desperately screaming at yourself to snap the hell out of it and get back in the driver's seat and do whatever it takes to regain control… isn't it ironic that this is what it took for me to understand how my parents must have felt in losing control?

The next day, however, I awoke without even the vague

hint of a hangover, so I foolishly declared that experiment half-successful; I know better now (as I painfully recall the excruciation of hangovers past while typing this) — much, much better.

It didn't stop there. This false courage extended even to my schoolwork. There was a particular subject which was my absolute favourite in that year. In my enthusiasm and an ill-conceived notion, I decided I could will my body to not sleep for two nights in a row, walk into that examination, and ace it. I saw myself getting one hundred percent on this paper, and I believed people were too timid to imagine they could achieve such things.

I did stay up for those two nights straight. I did walk into that exam with more confidence than all others. And I did crash in the middle of the paper as all the knowledge I had of the subject just magically, tragically slipped away.

It is scientifically proven that sleep deprivation has the same effect as drinking too much, and there is no analogy I love better than that as it shows how connected my wilfulness was to this type of absurdity. I wanted to be in control of my own free will so much that I would defy all logic and even science in trying to achieve it.

I failed that exam, in my favourite subject, and that

was the end of my mind-over-matter experiments. I stopped drinking my syrup-consistency cups of coffee, I began to research the effects of sleep on the brain, and I took a scientific approach to all of my superhuman decisions thereafter. Although when I repeated the course, I could only hope to get a passing grade no matter how high I scored, I chose to teach myself the lesson thoroughly by studying as though I could make the highest possible grade. I slept for eight hours before the exam, and while I did not get that full hundred, I satisfactorily scored in the nineties.

A New "Religion"

My Jamaican boyfriend and I didn't last. There were a few unfortunate events, the privacy of which I must respect at this time, that profoundly impacted each of our lives. Our couple of years together (my second and third years of university) taught me so much about navigating dualities, but in the end, it turned out that everything didn't have to be wrong for love to be wrong (eventually). Still, I had experienced my first "real" relationship, and while my maturity was a bit slow in that department, I found myself far more confident in my school work.

I graduated with an Upper Second-Class Honours (Weighted GPA 3.00 – 3.59 in equivalence) in my B.Sc. degree, and I was both extremely proud and disappointed by that: proud, knowing what I had endured, but disappointed, knowing I could have done so much better. I focused on what would come next: the pursuit of my PhD, which began with an M.Phil Programme while working as a teaching/ research assistant in engineering. Finally, my researcher dreams could begin.

It was around this time that the reliability of my studies and the nature of my curious mind led me to an intriguing concept: what if science could be my religion? I thought back to the way the knowledge within my textbooks comforted me through my first heartbreak and the fact that every time I had relied on a scientific approach, I had experienced a much higher chance of success. This safe predictability led me to wonder whether a belief in this "God" that humans spoke of was really necessary to navigate life.

I was never an atheist, especially not after all I had personally witnessed in my younger years, but I did lean into the path of being both agnostic and stoic. I did not know whether God existed, especially in the way He had been represented to me by religion, and I took issue with the expected sacrifice of freedom while being sold the dream of free will. I also began to question the ascribing of gender to a Being who represented all things, and the entire logic of a life spent in pursuit of the views of those who had placed themselves in authority over the church.

Yet, I did not want to be without a value system or principles of some kind as I feared the untethered choices I observed myself making in weakened moments. Stoicism felt like the balance I longed to have. A quick Wikipedia reference for those unfamiliar with the term: "It is a philosophy of personal ethics informed by its system of logic and its views on the natural world. According to its teachings, as social beings, the path to eudaimonia (happiness, or blessedness) is found in accepting the moment as it presents itself, by not allowing oneself to be controlled by the desire for pleasure or fear of pain, by using one's mind to understand the world and to do one's part in nature's plan, and by working together and treating others fairly and justly."

I perceived, however, that to free yourself from such control required a commitment to discard any connection to pain in favour of [an albeit repressed] indifference. My unaddressed trauma found solace in the words of Epictetus, a stoic Greek philosopher, who said, "Permit nothing to cleave to you that is not your own; nothing to grow to you that may give you agony when it is torn away."

In this regard, I reassessed all that I once considered to be "my" own: *my* family, *my* friends, *my* religion, *my* expectations, and even *my* virginity; everything came under the microscope of stoicism. I began to desensitise myself from the trappings of both pain and pleasure and focused instead on what it meant to let life flow through me. Anytime a challenging moment appeared, rather than asking myself what it could teach me, I misapplied Epictetus' views: "If therefore, any be unhappy, let him remember that he is unhappy by reason of himself alone."

I began to beat myself up whenever I felt low, and a sweet sense of power rose more and more each time. It was as though I had become invincible. My past couldn't hurt me unless I let it. People couldn't hurt me unless I let them. While the things that might hurt weren't avoidable, I could stop them from taking up residence or even unnecessary, momentary space inside of me.

It was like forgiveness 2.0, WWJD-on-steroids, without any obligation to religion, nor any need to invalidate any other belief for the sake of mine. I had found what I believed was a balanced form of "religion," which I concluded was both scientific and logical, and within this belief system, I had what I desired above all else: absolute free will.

This "religion" also informed my course of studies, as at a point within my M.Phil., I had observed how detrimental a lack of project management skills was for other researching students. I used my stoic beliefs to easily let go of any attachment I felt in pursuing *my* PhD right away and decided to change the entire direction of my course of studies. While still working in engineering, I looked to a degree which I had no qualifying work experience to enter.

This M.Sc. in Project Management was within the engineering faculty, but students had to have at least half a decade's work experience and be pursuing projects that required this degree for advancement. I fought to be accepted while shielding myself from potential disappointment through my confidence in my "nonattachment" beliefs, telling myself that I would be fine no matter the result. Yet I celebrated, with a profound attachment to the results, when I gained the support of two of my favourite professors [I was blind to my convenience-based stoicism]. I entered the programme under an exception and also as the guinea pig for their reassessment of entry requirements. I knew that I just needed to try my best, even if the scope was beyond me, and this filled me with relief. I was further relieved knowing I had armed myself with my best possible chance [stoicism] of escaping any negative emotions from both the results of that degree and any experiences to come.

What Is Worth Your Life?

It was a brilliant belief system, albeit clumsily and erroneously applied. For the most part, it worked. It also coincided with a period in my life when I was single but desired to have a companion of sorts with whom I could share my findings. I didn't want anything serious, and I didn't care if it was open, so long as it was an honest connection. I had a male best friend at the time who also happened to be single, and we decided that keeping each other company would be a world of fun.

And it was! I loved this guy, even if it wasn't very romantic because it was so real and raw and unguarded. He had none of the chivalry a woman might desire, and courtesy was only ever engaged upon unavoidable obligation. He did not care to be fake or to pull the wool over anyone's eyes, and this was refreshing beyond comparison.

We were the kind of friends who signed up to do dumb things together, explored random concepts and shared life stories, got drunk and smoked Hennessey-dipped cigars while we deep-dove into tech concepts and ideas for a sci-fi future, and it was as perfect as a friendship mixed with companionship could ever be.

But perfect things tend not to stay perfect, despite Newton's laws, and in our case, this was because what was really in motion was an unseen darkness that ravaged his soul, unbeknownst to him or me.

It started with little things. One night, we might have drunk too much, and he snapped a little at something I said. Another time, there would have been a party, and he was particularly rough in his speech at the end. I wondered what came naturally to me: was this easy and open relationship becoming an emotionally charged one with two people in denial of those growing, oxytocin-induced feelings?

It probably was. But this wasn't that. And there was no moment I knew that more clearly than the first time he physically held and shoved me. We were arguing — yet another time, as arguments had increased in frequency — and, with an alcohol-fuelled lack of inhibition, he just exploded. My immediate horror and his instantly sobered regret were our two reactions. I wanted to know "what the hell was that?!" and he could only profusely apologise, again and again, citing the devil in the drink.

I outwardly portrayed my hurt, but I inwardly denounced my pain. I would not allow it to make me unhappy, because if I did, I would be choosing unhappiness… yes, this is what made sense back then to me [that misapplied stoicism]. It didn't hit me that this was an unhappy situation or even a scary occurrence, but rather that my reaction needed a stern-talking-to so I would not fall into a funk.

My "forgiveness" was instant. He seemed so overly concerned, and even a bit freaked, by the appearance of this demon that compassion overcame me. I found myself reassuring him that it was okay because I could not stand to see my best friend in humiliating shock. See, just like me, he had already battled a lot of inherent insecurities and pain from his past (and even circumstances in his present). We were close because we shared these things, and I believed I was stronger than he was in dealing with them. I put my concerns aside and upped his in priority.

And then, it happened again. Despite it not being the first time, the shock factor was still present, and the dissociation was real. I only allowed myself to connect the instances after the third, fourth, fifth time turned a line into a potential trend. I began to gather data while still prioritising his challenges. I asked myself so many questions in an attempt to diagnose the issue. When did it happen most? When he was drunk. Why would he begin drinking? When he was socialising… no, when he was stressed, and then chose to socialise. Why was he stressed? Because of all of those issues that are happening or have happened. Gosh, my best friend is so stressed that he's resorting to alcohol and then bursting into violence. He must be in so much pain. He doesn't know how to release it as I do. How can I help him through this?

It is difficult to write this. It is hard to think of yourself as smart because of all the pieces of paper that claim you are, and yet simultaneously see how absolutely imprudent and misguided your choices were. But I genuinely did believe that I would be a horrible, disloyal person if I abandoned my best friend in the middle of his suffering (and only his, because, as far as I was concerned, I had the fortitude to handle this). I didn't perceive myself to be among "those" abused women who stayed with abusive men. I had logically chosen to be here… right?

Even more than those fallacies, I didn't want to

become what I hated the most. I knew what it felt like to be rejected and shunned from when I had changed into someone my old Christian friends saw as dark in nature. To be judged and misunderstood and raked over the coals for it by a dispassionate community was not a fate I wished on anyone, much less him. I was the closest person to him, close enough to see, know, and now painfully feel his darkness. How could I turn my back on him after he had been there when I tried to work through mine?

Guilt is a tricky emotion, but it's shame that's the mastermind, as it tends to use guilt as a mask. I felt guilty when I even considered abandoning him, but my darkness was feeding a very singular hunger: a need to be punished. All the shame I felt from how I had left Christianity to the way I had lost my virginity to the way I had treated my parents… all of the self-hate I felt for the many times I had messed up, the embarrassment and humiliation from my peers, and the lowly way in which I viewed my worth when I chose free will over a divine purpose… all of it was still there, cracks deep within my foundation, hidden under a makeshift rug. Little did I know that the strong structure I thought I had built was about to break.

If shame is the fear that we are not good enough (in the

words of Dr Brené Brown), then this was my biggest, scariest demon. Believing I wasn't good enough meant believing that I didn't deserve love or friendship that wasn't abusive to my mind, my heart, or my body.

It only got worse. There was a time when he hosted a small party, and I was upset by his alcohol-influenced behaviour and wanted to leave. I likely sensed it was going to be one of *those* nights. He caught me just as I was grabbing my things in his room, and he entered enraged, slamming the door behind him. I explained that I just wanted to rest, I had classes and assignments due for my masters, and I thought of any other possible excuse I could give. He grabbed me and sent me flying back against the bed, but my body just missed it. Instead, my head hit the thick wooden bed frame, and I lost consciousness for a short while.

I only know this because as I slowly came back into a state of awareness, confusion overtook my mind. My heart was pounding. No… something was pounding my heart. In his extreme panic that I had, perhaps, died, he was cuffing my chest over and over again, shouting my name in an attempt to resuscitate me. The music downstairs was loud enough to drown this out.

I will never forget how far within myself I sank as

what should have been the pain of his fist reverberated only with lifeless, soundless kinetic waves through my body. I felt nothing except a numbing sense of peace for the first time in probably a year. I figured I could continue to pretend that I had died, and perhaps he would believe he had lost me, and then I would finally be free… free of the obligation to save him, free of the shame of my past, and if he kept hitting me long enough, free of existence itself.

It was a plan that filled me with hope, at least until someone entered to use the en suite in his room, thereby eliminating my way out. What happened next will be enough to tell you the profundities of my damaged heart and mind: my instinct, my immediate, compulsive instinct, was to protect him. Whoever had walked in would have seen him crouched over a seemingly lifeless body while he repeatedly hit it in a way that made no sense outside of one conclusion: I was in danger. Energy poured into my system, fuelled with fear of what would happen, fear of rumours and humiliation for him, fear that this could ruin his life…

My eyes flew open, and I lurched forward, and the shocked girl just stood there with an uncertain, lingering gaze, hand still on the doorknob.

"She drank too much and passed out!" he stammered,

and the girl looked to me for confirmation. I nodded, not out of fear of him, but out of love. To corroborate the story, I added, "I'm sorry for any mess you might see when you go in there," pointing to the bathroom door, hoping to remind her of the reason she had come into the room. It worked, and she smiled empathetically and moved on with her night.

I did stay that night, mostly because he begged me to, and also because I was too weak to go home, although I lived one street away. The entire ordeal had shaken us both, and it was in this moment that he knew he needed help. Whatever fear he felt when he thought he had lost me made him desperate to fight his demon. He asked me to help him work out a serious plan to combat it, to find a therapist, and to figure out how we could heal from this. He wanted us to be together, and while there was a time when I might have wanted the same (a friend who grew to be a boyfriend), I agreed only because I didn't know what else to say.

The next day, we awoke and the physical damage of the night before finally came to collect its payment in pain. My chest hurt with each breath, and I probably had a concussion, but my concern was his wrist. He had managed to fracture a small bone in his hand from the force with which he had repeatedly pounded on my chest. We had to get it x-rayed and put in a cast, and I chose to pretend that I felt physically okay, but not great, because of what I saw within his eyes. Seeing that he had fractured his hand in beating me caused an already-present depression to deepen. This was a man who did not believe his life was worth much anymore.

As controversial as it is to say this, while those abused are the victims and survivors, those who abuse tend to be the victims of something dark, tortured, and heavily undiagnosed. And their survival, everything it means to live a good or better life without causing pain to others or themselves, strongly depends on those who are qualified and apart from the situation, those who are willing to see these issues, diseases and disorders (anger management, alcohol or drug abuse, intermittent explosive disorder, depression, etc.) as potentially treatable.

I say this now because there may be someone reading this who has abused or is abusing someone they love, or otherwise, and I want you to know that seeking professional help is not a weakness. The only way to combat this part of yourself that I'm sure you hate is to begin the fight with knowledge (diagnosis) and distance yourself from the people who represent your triggers so that those treating you can make a difference. It isn't simple, and it can be a very long and arduous road, but the cycle has to end somewhere, and starting where it begins — with those who exhibit all forms of abuse and violence as a symptom — gives everyone a fighting chance.

The Point Of Brokenness

I wish this story, in its timeline, had a happy ending.

He did begin therapy, and he was diagnosed with depression. The alcohol had made it worse, and while we didn't know it at the time, my presence offered the opposite of help. He had developed a dependency on me, and I had a need to be the kind of friend that would never, ever leave someone in the depths of their despair. But this, *this*, was beyond me. I want to say I should have known that, but I didn't. I was still pretending to be a peaceful stoic inside.

A little while after, the opportunity came to go with a female friend to Barbados. It was the week before "Crop Over" there — their carnival — and my friend and I were working out in the university's gym. She had the wild idea of going, and we made a well-humoured deal: if we were able to get cheap tickets for a flight that very day, we would jump on a plane and head over for the week.

We followed through with the hopeless attempt, but the joke was on us: two cheap tickets appeared for a flight in just a few hours. I remember looking at her to see who would call this bluff first, but as we purchased the tickets, while wildly laughing at our insanity, all I felt was a burst of hope. I would finally be able to get some space for the first time since the violence had started, and this felt like the drop of water my internal desert desperately needed.

We rushed to our homes and packed, and only at the very last minute did I tell him that I was going, when I knew it was too late to stop me. I'd never felt so relieved to see a plane liftoff from the ground, completely cutting off his access.

When I arrived, though, I felt concerned, worrying about his state of mind. What if he had turned suicidal? What if my frivolous desire to get away would be to blame? I texted him so he would know I was okay and that I would be back by the end of the week. He could not deal with it. He kept calling and texting my phone each day, revolving between "I know you need a break, and you deserve one" to "I need you here, I'm going crazy, please change your ticket and come back now! Please!"

I would be on the phone for over an hour at times,

while the group not-so-patiently waited for me to disengage so we could head to the parties and enjoy the nightlife. Even while I was out, I worried for him and battled the guilt of my temporary abandonment. He was at his lowest, and here I was, leaving him to deal, so I could "party."

When I returned, I braced for his rage but instead, he embraced me with so much love that I felt perhaps things had changed. They had and they did, within me. It finally occurred to me that this shouldn't be my life, if only because of how much I dreaded returning to it. Shortly after this, another violent incident occurred, and the change within me was certain: I got out of the relationship altogether.

This might have been how our relationship formally ended, but it was far from how the terror did. Six months later, after the calling, messaging, and stalking tapered off, the friend I'd travelled to Barbados with said she was heading out for the final day of carnival celebrations in my country [Trinidad]. Finally feeling free-*ish* of my recent, dark past, I decided to go with her and observe the celebrations while she played with the band. At the end of a very peaceful and fun-filled day, out of the thousands of people we had seen, my ex appeared. There was a situation with a couple he and I both knew, and my friend and I chose to assist. When it was over and we were walking on, my ex started following us. My friend and I rushed to the car, but just as I pressed the button to unlock it, he reached us… and then yanked open the backseat door and jumped in.

My friend and I stood for a few moments outside the car, just staring at each other, contemplating what to do. He began reasoning with me, saying that he'd only jumped in so I would hear him out before I said no; he said the truth was that he had missed his ride back home (which was the direction we were heading in) as he had stayed back to help in the same situation. It was late, and he had no way of reaching home, and all he wanted, all he needed, was a drop. This is the tricky thing about love and care; you can redirect them into other emotions, but they don't magically disappear.

I contemplated the scenario, thinking back to all the times he had been violent. He had never really exhibited anything in front of others. My friend being with me felt like a trump card for safety, and she seemed comfortable with the notion of simply dropping him off, because we would be together.

To anyone who has ever had this type of contemplation, please know this: if you ever need to find ways to justify what naturally strikes you as an unwise and unsafe [read: **dangerous**] decision, please know that it is not the right choice. Put yourself in a position of safety before you consider anything else!

The danger we were in didn't reveal itself right away. As soon as we hit the road, he fell asleep, and relief flooded me… until he woke up just as we turned into the area he and I both lived in. He began asking me to drop my friend home first so we could talk, and as I explained that I was staying with her that night, his insistence and voice grew louder. Something within me whispered that I should text his brother to be on standby, and as I hid my phone on the side and did this, I prayed — yes, *prayed* — that his brother would be at home.

By the time we pulled into his street, he was shouting obscenities at the top of his lungs. His brother was already outside, but what little self-control my ex had left finally broke. He managed to get at my seatbelt, and before I knew what was happening, he had wrapped it around my neck from the backseat and begun to pull with all his might.

I don't remember too much in the chaos that followed, only flashes. My terrified friend was trying to stop him; his brother was hitting him in an attempt to loosen his grip; neighbours were coming out of their houses (though none came to help). As I struggled to find a way to get even the smallest gulp of air with the seatbelt now digging into my throat, it hit me: "I'm about to die… but I never fulfilled my purpose."

It is an eerie feeling, sensing death just around the corner. It wasn't like the time when he knocked me out, when I sank into a sense of peace from a situation I believed to be inescapable. As my sense of consciousness began to drift, I could no longer hear my friend's cries or his brother's shouts. Instead, I remember an enraged force flowing into me. I wanted to live. I *needed* to live. I still had things to do, big things… divine things… and this would ***not*** be how my story ended.

Just as I felt this power, his brother managed to get in a blow that caused my ex's grip of the seatbelt to loosen. My friend got it from around my neck while his brother repeated his blows and dragged my ex out of the car.

"Drive!" my friend shouted, and I shoved my foot on the pedal, backdoor still open. In my rear-view mirror, my ex crawled along the road towards us, his brother holding him down as he screamed after the car.

CHAPTER FIVE

ROCKING ROCK BOTTOM

"The valley was not made for the weak," you muttered as you took another stumbling step to nowhere. You knew this, that you had to be strong, even despite the heaviness of your burdens and the darkness within your soul. It was a lesson you had learnt from the moment you left your birth mountain, ill-prepared for the path ahead. The valley was made for the bold and valiant, the strong and confident, the wise and knowledgeable… and, much to your despair, it appeared that you were none of these.

Not yet ready to face this hope-shattering reality, you focused on what you believed you could do, and do well, even if it was a pointless, stupid thing: climbing the tallest trees, and sometimes the most dangerous ones with rotting roots and cracked trunks that bowed to a nearing death. There was something familiar about their tippy-tops, despite the thick fogs that obscured all distant sight. Peace overtook you there in small amounts, and there were many nights that you fell asleep in the high branches.

It was a day after the most horrific, unspeakable event that you weakly climbed up the nearest tree. Nearing the top, you paused and hugged its trunk; the sobs broke out of your body and rolled into the fog. The tree shook with your weeping, sending a cascade of dead leaves down in the company of your freezing tears.

"I AM weak…"

It had finally hit you.

You weren't bold and valiant, strong and confident, wise and knowledgeable. You weren't remotely close to being any of those. Instead, you were a broken creature with darkness for a companion and terror for memories. You couldn't even remember why you left the comfort of your mountain, but you knew you no longer belonged there. You didn't belong here either, or anywhere.

Then, just as you were about to slide back down to

your life of despair, the faintest whisper travelled to you across the mist. It wasn't a familiar voice, not one you knew, yet its words sent strangely meaningful chills down your spine. You had perceived its intonations in every painful step, listened to it in both gurgling rivers and barren plains, but only when it chose to speak did you know what it was.

"Only those who know they are weak will find strength here. I was made for the weak so that they could become strong."

The Valley embraced you with the coolness of its winds and dampness of its fog, and while it was cold to the touch, comfort oozed into your pores. You sobbed once more, from the depths of your soul, but this time, your tears grew a little warmer.

Every Ending Is A Beginning

Everyone has a breaking point, but even in the chaos of rock bottom, the very occurrence of a breaking point means two sure things: the absolute, painful end of one part of the journey; and the jagged, jaded beginning of another.

It took a long time for me to stop feeling ashamed

that a flirtation with death was what it took for me to realise how much my life was worth living. In the months that followed, endless questions plagued my mind each day, with one resounding above the rest: where the hell was my survival instinct all that time?

I felt like a malfunctioning, short-circuiting, broken-without-replacement-parts human. Maybe I had been naïve enough to think the violence could never reach to that [near-death]. Perhaps it was through the looks of terror from my friend and my ex's brother that I finally saw the mess in which I had stayed. Even if the near-death experience had occurred six months after we ended, there was so much abuse built into the foundation before that final blow.

I began to blame myself. I hadn't been strong enough to leave him, strong enough to help him, or strong enough to save myself. I felt like a failure, more worthless than I had ever been before, and I surveyed my life for any possible way to counter that feeling. I turned to the one thing I believed I had left, the one thing I refused to fail at, even if it was to try to make myself feel better: my master's programme.

I had end-of-term examinations shortly after this experience, and I wasn't crazy enough to believe my grades would be unaffected. However, what I refused to allow, under any circumstance, was the loss of my overall A-average in my course. I figured that if I could somehow maintain it, that meant I wasn't completely useless and powerless… that I might be worth something yet.

I drowned myself in my work and studies, while developing a momentary and unhealthy relationship with a friend on the side in an attempt not to feel alone — as in, physically alone and unprotected from my ex, who still resided one street away. Yes, I had made a police report the night it happened and, for the record, the experience of this only made it far worse, due to what I have to assume was a severe lack of training in how to deal with victims/survivors of violence/abuse. Each time that I entered or left my apartment, all I felt was a damning fear that it could be my last moment.

I wanted only to be free. I wanted to walk through the university campus without looking over my shoulder every thirty seconds. I wanted to go out with my friends and not worry over who might appear from a dark corner. I wanted to perhaps even love again, without wondering if I would pay the ultimate price for moving on with my life. I found safety in this unhealthy connection, yet I also found myself lashing out with waves of fury at any hint of behaviour that could lead down the same path. I immediately ended it. This hypersensitivity and deep distrust in everyone, especially myself, wreaked havoc within me and likely leaked out to anyone close enough to feel my pain.

Each time I felt scared, I turned to my studies. Every time my heart skipped a beat when a passing face resembled my ex, I pounded more knowledge into my brain. He had taken everything from me, but not this, not yet, and I refused to let him. By the time the examinations came, I had two distinct states of being: work mode, and fear mode. In work mode, I was still a force to be reckoned with and laser-focused. In fear mode, I was a frail weakling who was irrefutably dumber than anyone in the world. I tried to stay in work mode as much as was humanly possible.

It may not have been the healthiest approach, but it helped beyond expression to see my A-average still existent at the end of that semester. Accomplishment took on a whole new meaning on the day of my results. With it came the vague memory of a line from my favourite book, The Chrysalids, in my high school Literature class: "I am not ashamed — I am only beaten." It made me believe that while I had been beaten into becoming a human failure, quite literally, only I could shame myself into remaining one.

Breathing Room Is A Fallacy

I had just oriented my viewpoint when I changed jobs (from the engineering faculty). In pursuit of a more targeted field in which to understand the scope of my masters in project management, I chose to gain experience in construction. Under the advice of the professor who would become my dissertation supervisor, I sought new skills and more insight within that industry. However, if I am honest, there wasn't much allure to it.

With a mind as fantastical as mine, I wanted to work on world-changing construction projects with new, even experimental, technology built into terrestrially challenging areas. This was not that — not quite. Still, as a means to an end, the end being increased understanding, it was worth the exploration.

It was there, in this new job, that I met the man who would become my son's father. I entered the company more than six months after the near-death experience, and this particular young man was assigned to set up my computer. We sparked up an easy conversation, and his intelligence instantly shone. He was soft-spoken yet witty, had dry humour mixed with an eloquence that I loved, and the connection was instantaneous. In our first month of dating, we talked and took things slowly, but in the second month, we decided to explore new and fun areas.

As fate would have it, despite using multiple methods of birth control, our doctor traced the date of conception precisely to the second time we ever had sex. Can you imagine what that must have felt like?! I was just starting to relax in my exploration of this new soul with a kind heart, while still wondering — deep in the back of my mind — how to heal from my recent past. And now, he and I were being hit with an inexplicable curveball that could only be the work of what I believed was a very ridiculous God.

Yet, when we found out, we took a drive to a beach along the north coast and decided to walk separately and think deeply about what we should do. It was in that moment, staring out at the sea's horizon, that I felt all the fear once again. How could I even consider bringing a life into this world when I barely knew who I was? How would I protect this new, innocent life when my very survival instinct had a severe malfunction? I also didn't understand how it was possible that I was in the 0.000000000001% [exaggerated] to be dealt this hand. What I did know, despite all my fears and rejection of divinity, was that I would be foolish to diminish the existential meaning of this to mere probabilities or chance.

When we returned to each other from our thought-walks, we had the same response: we are supposed to have this baby. Everything that had aligned for Alyxander (the Great) to be in this world, even the fact that I could have died mere months before, made me believe that his life was not only special, but powerful in its very existence. He had been willed into being, and we could not deny the divinity we each felt growing within me.

We called our folks shortly after to give them the news, and my mother said the words that any daughter in this position would be just as happy to hear: "don't you dare abort my grandchild!" As simple as that line was, and as complex and non-ideal as my situation was, it meant that she instantly accepted she was going to be a grandmother and, in a way, accepted me and my son. It so happened that by the end of that year, my parents returned home from Alaska — before my son was born. They believed it had to be divine timing.

The catch? Alyx's father and I were both in our early/mid-twenties, with minimal life experience and ridiculous expectations for what this would be like. Throw the raging pregnancy hormones and my past trauma into the mix, and it was the makings of a disastrous pregnancy experience.

While we did move to a new place, which helped the worries of my ex, new fears replaced my old ones. My hypersensitivity for any possible threat, amplified by the chemistry running through my system, was the perfect cocktail for sky-high walls and a need to conceal all vulnerability. I would convince myself, and him, that I had it all together. Then, when I crashed from faking strength, I raged with fears. The only thing that kept me anchored was my studies. I finished all my required courses successfully within my pregnancy, with only my dissertation left to complete.

While we tried our best, we weren't always good to each other, and we both accept that now with shaking heads and reminiscent smiles. I made most of my mistakes swinging between the superwoman who still aced exams while pregnant, and the broken-woman who suffered from codependency. For a man who was likely never sure when his woman *really* needed him, his most major mistake was treating my new and growing pain lightly. To be fair, it wasn't entirely his fault.

In my third trimester, I began to experience sharp bouts of pain, radiating in and around my womb, that I couldn't explain. It grew so terrifying one night that I woke him up to get me to the hospital. We went, but when they checked for contractions, there were none. I was livid, insisting I was in pain, but the nurses believed it was false contractions [read: a false belief in non-existent contractions]. One even pulled my partner aside and said that perhaps I had a low pain tolerance, and I was merely scared. This only worsened the perceived credibility of my suffering, and during the times the pain was inexplicably absent, I even began to question myself.

There's a lesson here, and it's a crucial one: you are the **only** one who can ever know what you're feeling and what you need. The challenge is becoming aware enough to know if that need is being sourced from a place of healthy or unhealthy fear, because a healthy fear can save your life. For a time, I ignored the pain as much as I could, wanting to appear strong and hating the embarrassment of my previous hospital experience. I despised how he looked at me — like the weakling who couldn't handle herself — so I built an even greater façade of strength.

This worked fairly well, at least until the night when the pain hit with such magnitude that I was helpless in its wake. He wasn't entirely motivated to get me to the hospital, but this time I didn't care. By the time we arrived, I was throwing up in convulsions, and the nurses, finally concerned, reached out to my doctor. My incredible doctor, equally enraged, ordered that they scan my organs, and it was then that they discovered my gallbladder was full of small gallstones and prepping itself for a machine-gun-esque eruption. I had to be rushed into surgery to remove my baby boy, and in hopes that it was the pregnancy hormones that had caused the gallstones to appear, we kept my gallbladder in for observation. The hope was that the stones would dissipate with the hormones, and I would get to keep my organ.

Having had another dance with danger, I knew this one thing for the first time in years: I needed to figure out how to trust myself again. Sometimes you need a powerful catalyst to tune in, to listen, and mine had just arrived.

A Reason To Live

There is nothing, *nothing*, like holding your tiny human in your arms and knowing that his little life depends significantly on how you choose to live yours. Of all the things that I wanted him to experience through me, I wanted to show him what limitless living looked and felt like by my example.

His father and I, lacking the healthy couple foundation to raise our baby together, decided after a series of upsets to part relationship-ways and co-parent. Alyxander was just four months old. While painful in the experience of it, I knew this was the right thing to do: if I couldn't give my son a family filled with more love than persistent conflict, I would give him all the love I had as a single mother and co-parent. I was well aware that I couldn't be a new mother, working full-time and writing my dissertation, while trying to figure out how to contribute to a relationship I didn't believe had much hope. Whether my past experiences of men fuelled that feeling could indeed be argued, but in those moments, I chose to trust the only part of this equation which I could influence: me.

We eventually worked out a system to ensure Alyxander knew our love and families, but it was a minefield to navigate for a while. As had become my modus operandi, I self-soothed by diving into my studies with a new single focus: obtaining an 'A' in my dissertation so I could attain a distinction in my masters. I saw this as my first gift to my son in alignment with what I believed it meant to be limitless. As my research progressed with each new baby tooth and laugh and word, a 'new' physical pain surfaced within me. I didn't realise for a while that it was my gallbladder once again (pregnancy displaces organs a bit), but when my suspicions increased with the level of the intermittent pain, this time *I* wilfully chose to ignore it. As to why I insisted on learning this lesson the hard way, stubbornness is as much of a curse as it can be a gift. It wasn't for the wrong reasons, though — just not the right ones.

I could see the finish line for my tumultuous masters. After having almost lost my life during it, I believed I could only close that chapter — the abuse, the worthlessness, the fears — when I had incontrovertible proof that I hadn't been broken beyond repair. Each time the pain waves began, I rocked myself to sleep in a fetal position and cried until it passed. Then, when it did, I got up and started the cycle again.

It was irrational, and it was dangerous. I can only give thanks for the grace that carried my stubborn focus to the finish line. When my dissertation was finally handed in, with its 'A' in sight, it was Alyxander's father who found me on the floor in my apartment, writhing in pain, and rushed me to the hospital. My parents arrived shortly after, showering me with all the support in the world while gently reprimanding me for ignoring the pain. The surgeon removed my gallbladder in the nick of time, saving me from the eruption and gifting me with a small container of over twenty gallstones.

In my attempt to prove I could be limitless, I had

come face-to-face with a limitation that not even the strength of my will could conquer: my humanity, in the form of my body. I believe we are given these vessels of flesh to remind us that there are ways to use our gifts that can either honour our bodily existence or take advantage of it — well, attempt to, anyway. The truth is, plagued by the insecurity of being a twenty-four-year-old single mother who had failed at so many things, I just needed to succeed at this *one* thing. It wasn't a healthy need, not at its root, and it cost me an entire organ.

I had attached my worth to everything other than merely my existence on the planet. When all of these constructs fell, from my virginity onwards, so too did the value I placed on myself. Gaining my masters through those difficult circumstances had undoubtedly reassured me that I still had what it took to become something meaningful, but it was when I gazed upon my son the first time after the surgery that it all changed. I faced the risk I had taken by gambling my life for a piece of paper that could have left my one-year-old motherless. It was time to get a handle on my life.

Who Are You?

I despise this question in job interviews. How could anyone hope to get an answer to one of the most complex questions on the planet in mere seconds? Yet, as complex as it was, I believed that getting a hold of my life began here. I had set out on a journey outside of Christianity to figure out who I would have been without all of my childhood conditioning, but, in evacuating my foundation, I had instead allowed everything and everyone around to condition me. It hadn't been intentional on their parts or mine, but it had become my reality. And it needed to change.

During this period, I had stumbled across the work of Carl Jung and the continued research of Katherine Cook Briggs and her daughter, Isabel Briggs Myers, which resulted in the introspective self-report questionnaire that helped people to understand their personality types. It was called the Myers-Briggs Type-Indicator (MBTI), and it was a fascinating discovery to make at the time.

Using the questions as guideposts, I was able to get a very clear view of my behaviours by examining what I practically did in life's circumstances (versus what I would like to think I would do if given a choice). It was as honest as

I could get with myself, and my results blew me away. Almost every word of it resonated within me. To examine this theory even further, I sent the test to everyone in my life. Each person responded with the same general exclamations about how eerily accurate the results were and how much more they understood themselves.

A light had come on inside me, and I could finally observe the inner workings of my mind. I began to see connections to decisions I had made in the past and reasons that the many methods I had tried for sculpting out my person wouldn't work. I wasn't a common personality type, especially for a woman, and not only did that mean that being misunderstood was my fate, but it also meant I had very few reference points (other women like me) to help me understand myself.

Still, I wasn't intimidated. I felt more hope than I had since I began my journey. This hope was only deepened by two diverse but powerful books I had read during that time: The Alchemist by Paulo Coelho, and The Brain That Changes Itself by Dr Norman Doidge.

Dr Doidge's book broke down the scientific concept of neuroplasticity, which is the study of changing brains — the idea that my brain, and yours, "can change its own structure and function through thought and activity." Someone reading this may think, "well, duh" but for a long time, we perceived the brain as fixed, except during the malleable childhood years when babies and little children learn everything from language to mobility, and their personalities become set in 'tissued' stone. Practically speaking, this once meant that a child with a low IQ would never get smarter, those with compulsive obsessions would never have another life story, and even those with phantom limbs would be stuck like that for the rest of their lives.

Neuroplasticity debunked these myths with a view to ending the misrepresentation of, arguably, our most powerful organ. Dr Doidge explored case studies which ranged from curing stroke patients to raising IQs to rejuvenating ageing brains. He even shared case studies on the neural effects of pornography and sexuality, on how a woman born with half a brain can wholly function, and on a solution to a vision-impaired individual. And, above all else, he showed me that the science had proven I was only stuck in my muck by ignorant choice.

The Alchemist, the other powerful book, is a book you should not read just once. I'm convinced that when I'm sixty, I'll have an entirely fulfilling yet different experience in reading it all over again. The first time I read it, during that period, there was an Arabic word that had such impact on me, I felt I needed to have it tattooed on my body [I haven't — yet?]. This word was "Maktub," and it stands for "it is written." In The Alchemist, it was a word of trust in everything as it unfolded, believing that God had written all, and so we must confidently walk the path with this knowing. Some rode towards certain death with this word, cherished lovers were left behind to fulfil a purpose with this word, and all it took was to know that an unfolding reality was also a fated one.

For the adult life I had lived thus far, there was much to be said about the reality I had unfolded, but in reading those words, I had a passing thought that perhaps it was for a purpose I couldn't see, and certainly couldn't yet understand. Had I been meant to endure such a horrid journey, and if so, to what end? I didn't have the answer, but I latched on to the feeling of a tiny glimmering beauty in my pain.

And, finally, in this search for who I was outside of the conditioning of my upbringing, one thing stood out above all the rest: every night, while tucking my son to sleep, I sang him a lullaby — "You Are My Sunshine" — and said a prayer… a Christian prayer. Some part of me was unwilling to risk bringing my son into my exploration of faith and the very existence of God. It was because, despite everything that had happened, there was a value to my childhood that could not be eclipsed or diminished, and I wanted my son to have it in the only way I could give that was honest and sincere. Embracing this understanding had a significant impact, later on driving a choice to allow my parents to add greatly to his spiritual — and educational — foundation.

Spirituality mattered to me, to who I was, even outside of religion. There was something beyond the known realm of science that called to the abyss within me. Unfortunately, I didn't quite know how to answer.

Choosing My First Mark

I did get a tattoo, but it was one that pre-existed every other dream, one that represented a secret I had felt drawn towards since I was a little girl: it read "Bios Lumen," the Greek and Latin root words of "bioluminescence" and they roughly translated to "Living Light." In the back of my mind, my dreams of becoming a research scientist still very much existed, and with them was the study of bioluminescence and its applications, which I believed could add so much to the world.

The realisation of these dreams wasn't quite so simple anymore. I now had a son, and I didn't have the means to provide for him and pay for a doctoral programme from a reputable university for which I would temporarily need to migrate. To that end, I decided to try to pursue a very rare scholarship and let the results decide whether now was still the time to follow these dreams. I proposed my thesis to explore, in essence, the use of bioluminescence in the study of Alzheimer's as a non-invasive technique for understanding how the disease functions, and the day I wrote my GRE, I went straight to the tattoo parlour to demarcate my commitment.

The words meant far more than the actual pursuit. The concept of living creatures being able to produce their light, from fireflies and certain mushrooms to the vast range of aquatic creatures, meant that existentially, perhaps we all could. And even if that light didn't burn with the warmth and luminance of the brightest sun, it could still light its path and send a message to those meant to receive it.

My son was turning two a few months after I marked my passion on my body, and it was also around this time that I dated a guy who would gift me with a rare kind of love that extended fully to my son. He kept me company at the tattoo parlour and supported whatever illustrious dreams I had with a belief in me that felt unbelievable. It took me a while to accept it was real. This guy had been a friend of my extended family for a long time, so much so that he would be present at family weddings. I didn't pay much attention to him until I noticed his involvement in music: he was a rhythm guitarist for an island rock band, and an avid consumer of all things rock music. Yet, despite the stereotype some of you are painting in your heads, he wore the most colourful clothes, loved to laugh, and was the least emo person I knew. He also loved all things carnival and had a healthy appetite for video games and nightly anime and cartoons.

It admittedly took me a few months to allow him into my heart. I had had a very short exploration with someone before him, and it had shown me that I was far from ready to take anyone seriously as, to me, most people weren't serious. Aside from this new guy's lighthearted ways amplifying my jadedness, I also held deep insecurities about being a young, single mum. I figured that no guy in his right mind would want to entangle himself with a woman who had a child (and by extension, a child's father) in tow. Even more than that, I was unwilling to risk anyone being a serious part of my life without loving my son as if he were his own.

The night came when my son woke up with a fever, sending me into a state of new-mum-panic. I reached out to my mother, and she called up our family doctor, who lived an hour away. [My incredible parents became my village in so many ways, it deserves a book of its own!] I had likely texted my guy to let him know my plans, but as I packed up my son to leave, I heard a vehicle pull up outside my apartment; it was him. Insistent that I not drive alone or drive at all so that I could be with my son in the backseat, he had jumped into action with just as much panic as I had felt, yet with the presence of mind to offer a valuable solution I didn't know I needed. For me, our relationship officially started that night, when he stepped up without being asked, showing magnanimous care for the life and well-being of my son.

Still, life was far from perfect. A global recession had taken place, and this cost me my job in construction. I tried to start my first company, but failed and disappointed my business partners and myself. Eventually, I ended up in a science and technology state agency, running an innovation and invention unit, and this sparked some hope; it felt closer to my research dreams. It was a period of professional upheaval, but it also felt like I was being protected and guided in ways I couldn't quite comprehend.

Our relationship lasted a couple of years, and it was also not perfect. His youth still in hand, he made choices that weren't aligned with my developing value system. However, it was seeing myself begin to want more and need more, in the areas of principles and belief systems, that made me realise my work on myself had started to amount to something. His habit of lying helped me understand how much I valued the truth. His capacity to quickly bounce back from even the worst of moods allowed me to identify this as a quality I desired. His then-inability to explore the roots of the moods showed me that I wanted something deeper. His very present and demonstrative love for my son helped me form a standard for anyone to be a meaningful and permanent part of my life. His absolute avoidance of exploring conflicts and their repeated patterns showed me that I had become more willing to face a bit of my darkness… but he wasn't.

It was a beautiful season, reason, and lesson, and it is one I have never regretted. However, of all the gifts that this relationship gave me, there was one I wasn't aware of at the time, a seed like no other: my cautious return to music.

Flirting With Sound

You can't run from your deepest roots. These aren't the ones biologically given to you by nature/birthing, or even your childhood/upbringing. These are connected to who you are here to be and what you're here to do. While I abstained from creating music, I found myself managing the business of it for my guy's rock band. And I resisted it with a passion.

Parts of me felt like I was flouting the self-imposed rules of my departure from Christianity. I had also been taught that rock music was a special brand of "devil music" and this hitched a ride in my brain while I processed whether I should even get involved. Still, as I listened and witnessed the band's songwriting process and the passion they put into their unique sound, I sensed nothing evil about it. They were creative in ways that made me miss my days of music to the point of pain.

After being pressured into the responsibility, I accepted it mostly because I believed they deserved a real chance at this and I wanted to help in any way I could. I began exploring the business workings of the industry and familiarised myself with the processes needed for their unique case. And I fell in love with it. This was a hidden and safe intersection between my disparate worlds in which I could play with and explore my undying love for music. It was only on the side, but supporting my guy and his friends in their mission to bring this music to the world was the experience of love in all its forms.

Even after the relationship ended, I remained their manager for a while, as per their request, and I support their musical endeavours to this day. How could I not? Even without the incredible music, this gift they gave me was a giant piece of the puzzle: our callings are our own. They aren't contingent on circumstances or choices, and they are above the noise of our becoming. While all of this only made sense in retrospect, it was through it that I found the breadcrumb trail that would lead me back to a precious and vital part of me.

The Point Of Turning

The only time we should turn back is when we are turning into ourselves. It is both a choice to turn our views from an outward to an inward perspective and a choice to become who we always were and are meant to be. Turning points are the ways we can rock rock-bottom. And yes, there's a lot of head-banging, guitar-smashing, top-of-lungs screaming that may have to take place, but if it results in a meaningful pivot to our insides, then it's worth all of the noise.

In these moments, these points of clarity, who I was began to take shape. I could see the milestones appearing in front of me, stepping stones I was leaping onto in order to reach my dreams — applying for the PhD scholarship, finding trust in myself, and even embracing music once again. My life seemed to be taking on a restorative alignment, like the clouds clearing after a storm.

You might have noticed, however, that there is no "Dr" in front of my name at the time of this writing, and I say it this way not because it is in progress, but because I know better than to speak for Future-Me. I didn't get that scholarship. And, at the time, I didn't find it within me to embrace music again. I sang only once, at my grandmother's funeral [it was one of her requests], and then tucked away my grieving voice once more.

In the midst of this, a Bible story came back to me, that the Israelites, having been delivered from Egypt by Moses, spent forty years wandering the desert before reaching the Promised Land. God had cursed them so that a journey which should have taken days instead took a generation.

The reason for the curse? Well, after all the works and miracles that God had shown them, when the twelve spies were sent to assess the new land/ home for the people, they returned with reports fuelled by fear and doubt. The people chose to believe in and spread this hysteria, rather than trusting in the will of God. The price for their lack of faith was a dreadful delay in the fulfilment of a divine promise.

If I were to believe in the concept of "maktub," that all of this was already written and the story was the mere unfolding of the divine lessons encapsulated, then this is both a warning and a form of wisdom.

The warning? There is a price to pay for pushing away your calling.

The wisdom? If you're paying the price, it was fated for a divine reason you may one day discover, and for that reason, your shortest distance will not be a straight line.

CHAPTER SIX

THE SHORTEST DISTANCE IS <u>NOT</u> A STRAIGHT LINE

Perhaps you'd always known it, perhaps it was held captive in places hidden from your spirit, but when the Valley spoke to you, you recognised its truth in the core of your being. This truth hadn't ended your wandering, which still had no clear direction, but it became a strange and comforting companion.

Together, you took steps and missteps, but every time you fell in the darkness, a hand extended to help you stand again. You often refused it. And so, a new, shorter cycle began. You fell, you lamented, you twisted in mud, claiming this was the last of you, and shouted to the darkness to take you.

You slapped away the hand repeatedly, until you found that it always remained extended, ready to bring you back to the naked comfort of truth. You got up.

You fell again, you lamented, you claimed it was your last bit of hope, and you slapped the hand away, but this time only once before you grabbed on. Then, you fell again, you lamented, you felt hopeless, but you didn't linger there. You immediately held the hand when it appeared. Soon, you found yourself simply falling and lamenting, and then tucking and rolling hand-in-hand with truth, until every fall took on a ridiculous hilarity — at least until one day, when it occurred to you that you had been falling in the same spot.

But how was that possible? Perhaps it only felt familiar because of the number of times you had fallen. You got up, truth at your side, and kept walking, but this time you took notice of the bowing tree with the diamond etching, the fallen rocks by the small cave, the unique curvature of the stream that insisted on following a figure-eight before moving along… and then, you saw it.

The exact dip in the ground, just as you came closer to the bowing tree with the diamond etching, now right in front of you. Awareness rocked you like an earth-shattering quake. You had been walking in a gigantic circle over and over again all this time!

You broke into tears, the absolute pointlessness of it all hitting you in torrents. In horror, you continued in your circle, just to be sure, past the fallen rocks by the small cave and the stream with the figure-eight in its path, and it was there you stopped, knelt on its banks and let out a bloodcurdling scream from the depths of your being. Then, when it was all out, and you had sat there for a time beyond time, you pushed yourself up and stared at your reflection in the waters.

It was then that you saw yourself for the first time since you had left your birth mountain. You were older, as though the milk had drained from your face and pain had taken its place, and you were bruised and scraped in so many places, you couldn't count them. Determined to see what you had become, you removed every article of tattered clothing adorning your body and took a quick glance at your most naked form. What you saw amid the marks of trauma was something you had never seen or been, before — your form was now sleekly clad in long, lean, powerful muscles.

You had become stronger.

And then, as if on cue, a song from a past lifetime reached your ears as the fogs began to part, sending reminiscent chills through every cell in your body:

"The world needs you to come home to your mountain. When will you come to find me?"

You May Not Know What You Want, But You Can Start With What You Don't

Experimentation isn't in everyone's core design, but it is certainly in mine. It was why Ecclesiastes was my favourite book in the Bible, why I wanted to be a research scientist, and why I loved disproving my life-hypotheses so I could be one step closer to my truth. That was my sole intention — to find my truth — and for me, it was the only point of this kind of exploration. If it wasn't purposeful, it wasn't valuable.

After having experienced a relatively good relationship with my ex, yet still finding myself dissatisfied (existentially) by no fault of his, I began to wonder what exactly I wanted in a companion. It was an easy list to start — honesty, faithfulness, no abuse, for example — but it was a difficult one to finish.

A seemingly simple question I would ask myself was, "do I want someone ambitious?" and the immediate answer would be yes. The next question, though, was tricky: "what should he be willing to sacrifice, and not sacrifice, for that ambition?" He should be willing to sacrifice his fears — yes — but he shouldn't sacrifice his integrity for opportunities — a big no-no. He should be willing to sacrifice some quality time — yes — but not so much that the quality of our connection would waver — a big no-no.

A follow-up question to that would also be, "what should, and shouldn't, be the intentions behind his ambition?" To get rich? To be popular? To fulfil a lifelong dream? To follow his calling? To prove something? To provide for his family? A combination of these, or none of them? And if a combination, as most people are, what ratio would feel aligned with my developing value system? By now, you're likely getting the point. Apply this thought process to every single characteristic you can imagine, and what came from this wasn't a list, but a mental drawing.

Either way, it didn't take me very long to realise that people don't wholly abide by lists or even personality types. They are full of curveballs and holes, and most aren't exactly lining up to ask themselves why. It was frustrating, as I believed everyone to be innocent until proven guilty, so I would take them at their word until that word was broken. I tried to understand the reasoning behind us humans finding ourselves incapable of being the people we wanted others to believe we were. Why claim to be something that you weren't, say, fifty percent of the time? I realised that we're mostly glass-half-full when it comes to representing ourselves, and why shouldn't we be? Who else will think the best of us, if not us?

Love is a very complex experiment, and with people not following their own rules and my lists failing to be comprehensively helpful, I decided to stop the maddening pursuit of something with permanence. Instead, I chose to take it down a notch, and simply date.

Pass-The-Time Relationships

It sounds worse than it is, really, but it was the name a girlfriend and I gave to our dating approach. We had both come out of serious relationships around the same time, and we decided that while the emotions of dating would be very real, we would remind each other if/when things ended that our mission had been a lighthearted one. With the pressure removed to find "The One," I could easily experiment using an elimination method: determine more and more of what I didn't want through this one-by-one experience of humans so that I could reduce the scope of potential future mates. And, for the icing on the cake, should one of these men turn out to be precisely what my soul had searched for, we could build something beautiful while I sent my experiment into retirement.

Someone is reading this right now, shaking their head at my approach, but for someone (me) who hadn't exactly had a great relationship trajectory, you'd be surprised at how much safer this felt. I avoided allowing anyone to get close to my son — rule number one — and I gave each guy the fairest chance possible, redirecting my jadedness with the reminder that this was a meaningful experiment. I allowed myself to feel all of the love and intrigue that each person evoked, and I also allowed myself to feel all of the pain when their masks cracked with a little time. I was also very candid about the person I was discovering myself to be, from the Myers-Briggs personality typing — which I asked each person to do at the start — to my evolving values and views of the world.

Some loved the belief system I was building, at least in theory. In practice, when they found that I had pulled away after having discovered gross misalignments, they viciously attacked what they had claimed to love. For wanting complete honesty, I was told I was unreasonable because "everyone lies." For having high standards of faithfulness, I was told to "get with the times" and stop being "insecure."

I didn't understand it. I would enter these connections being so upfront about who I was and what I hoped to experience. I would explain my value system and ethical beliefs, and ask them about theirs to see whether there was a workable intersection. I figured that if our values weren't aligned, these experiments were doomed from the start. Every single person I had this conversation with all said a version of the same thing: that our values were incredibly aligned and that they had been longing to find a woman who held these beliefs. And, when it finally showed that either their self-awareness was flawed, or it had all been lip-service, I would be to blame for wanting the connection to end. Why? Because I wouldn't lower my standards to accommodate their choices.

The irony? I hadn't begun to raise my standards from the basics to the second stage of my experiment. This had all just been in the areas of honesty, faithfulness, kindness, and anger management.

For four years, I performed the same experiment in the hopes that, having narrowed my scope with each interaction, I would find a different response and a better fit. All I ended up with was discouragement. I began to feel like it wasn't just marriage that wasn't for me; it was any form of a meaningful and lasting connection.

There were a couple of connections within this period that did hold deep meaning for me. I had allowed myself to love, and even without finding what I had hoped for, I had still found incredible men on awe-inspiring missions for their lives. With the couple of them who moved me, I often wanted to find a way to be a less intense individual than I was, so that I could justify their repeated choices with their accompanying "I'm sorry, I won't do it again." But despite my best efforts, I couldn't stay "less" for long.

The challenge was me. I had paid the past price of lowering my standards and drifting without clear values in the most heart-shattering, body-abusing, mind-traumatising ways. Every time I tried to convince myself that I could be laxer with one of my values, I would feel the inexplicable crash within me, and numbness began to take hold again. I was failing myself, failing my healing, failing my progress, and it would burn a hole through my soul. A listlessness would sweep in as I found myself trying to accept more and more of them while becoming less and less of me.

Then, as if in complete revolt for my steps down the familiar, dark path of my unbecoming, every part of me would reject this misalignment with a fury. This "switch" was irreversible, and my inclination to stay would drain away. In its place, I found the strength to embrace an unavoidable end wholly. And then, the cycle repeated.

Pass-The-Time… Careers?

Believe it or not, this is probably both the least fitting and most fitting way to describe my career path. As a ship that had set out to sea, with a captain who had lost the map after being in the direct path of a storm, I was now clueless as to what should come next. My research scientist dreams were shelved, and the most I could do was try to connect with the peripheries and shadows of those dreams.

Here's the truth I learnt through this: **to return to the path of your becoming, you must first return to yourself.** But this self isn't the person you were when you first ventured down the darker twists of your journey. *You're* not the same person you were, so it may feel like you are starting from scratch.

This would be easier if there weren't still many, MANY echoes of who you used to be interlaced with the person you now are. Deciphering the Present-You versus the Past-You is like trying to disarm a trick bomb — it just doesn't work in the way you'd think. You're far more likely to find yourself dancing in the explosion, turning into a fantastical animal, passing out from the stink of the smell, or generally being disoriented in some way than you are to find yourself actually blowing up.

The answer to the question, "what am I here to do?" was an elaborate trick bomb of this very nature. I would try to cut a wire here or there and find myself doing a dance I'd never signed up for with a company I didn't believe in (or work I didn't believe in), and then I'd try again. My saving grace through this was viewing them all as a play on those same pass-the-time relationships, except with an aim to narrow the scope of what I was here to do by getting clearer on what I wasn't.

Again, that isn't to say that these varied fields weren't valuable to my journey and my knowledge. Each one gave me an opportunity to hone a new set of skills, and a range of experiences that I would never have had otherwise. I engaged in everything from engineering to construction to science and technology to innovation and invention to project management to procurement. However, it was the paths I created for myself that were the most fulfilling.

If The Shoe Doesn't Fit, Consider Becoming A Shoemaker

The second company I created (on the side of my regular job) was catalysed by my stint with my ex's rock band and my exposure to the business of music. A desire had been birthed inside me and if I couldn't be in music, I would help those who were to find ways of making their paths sustainable.

I started on my journey with the first aim being to provide a more regular performing space and opportunities for artistes to use that space. I got an opportunity to organise such a movement at a local venue. While I didn't have the means to invest entirely into it, I worked out a profit-sharing arrangement with the more established artistes, while allowing selective spots for the newer artists who wanted a chance to display their talents.

It was an intimate affair, with a small committee of incredible humans, but it became the shining part of my weekly routine. Even at my regular job, I invited those I worked with to come and partake in the enjoyment of brilliantly composed and performed local music. A few of those co-workers became regulars on the Tuesday night sessions, which wrapped up early enough for us to all get a good night's sleep.

It was in this created work that I found a connection to a purpose I didn't know existed. I started to have deeper conversations with those in the music industry regarding their challenges, and I longed to figure out how I could contribute to making their passions prosper. The more I held these talks, the more fractured the industry seemed, but with those fractures came ideas for what I could do to help. Still, it needed to start at a national policy level for this to make sense, so when an incredible industry friend insisted that I apply for a position like this within a state agency, I sent my curriculum vitae and put it to the back of my mind.

Meanwhile, my regular job became more engaging as it started to deal with procurement systems, and not seemingly disconnected tasks. I loved system building for the purpose of either problem-solving, or the creation of new forms. This new area seemed to have elements of both. As the summer stint of my local music events ended with a fantastic concert featuring one of my favourite local bands, Freetown Collective, I began to transfer the fundamentals of system-building in procurement into my understanding of the wider music industry.

Our market was too small, as a Caribbean island, to sustain artistes and musicians in the way I envisioned they could be, and there wasn't enough collaboration between the other creative industries in my view. Intrigued, I decided to have a second series of events a few months later, collaborating with another company to bring this to life: local fashion, art, music, anime, storytelling, culture, and select products, all in one space.

I figured that a combined marketplace could encourage a broader, shared market for these creatives. They could sell their creations, get paid for performances, display their work, and meet others like them who were all fighting the same fight. My then business partner and I gave a lot of ourselves to this, despite other obligations. All seemed to be aligned, both the night stars and the creative stars. Yet, just a couple of days before the launch, a curveball like no other smashed into me.

The person arguably in charge of the place where I worked (my regular job) saw me in the studio for an interview with a local TV station about the movement to support these creatives. He decided, notwithstanding the fact that there was no conflict of interest with my job, that after this interview I was to report to HR due to a contract clause that said he must approve any of my activities outside of working hours.

Although I had never taken a day off nor ever been late for work to make these contributions to the industry, and despite having declared my work openly — though, perhaps, not formally — in the creative industries which predated this job, my employers told me in no uncertain terms that if I launched my events, they would take action against me.

It felt like an impossible situation. I had just been on the TV talking about it that very morning. I had signed contracts with participants. I had sent in all the information I possibly could regarding the intention of the events and my passion for helping the industry. I even tried asking my workplace for just two months to fulfil these obligations, and then I could adhere to their directives. The answer was no.

I had no nest-egg; it was a December, with Christmas just weeks away and lots of gifts in line to purchase for my son. Even my vehicle was tied to the company through a loan they had facilitated.

Suddenly, I was face-to-face with a make-or-break decision: either keep the absolute comfort of my job and salary and vehicle, while enjoying my free time instead of investing it into developing a very tough creative sector, or jump off a cliff towards what I believed was a part of my purpose, but with no sponsors, no support, and no clue as to how the hell I was going to sustain myself — just like these very creatives I longed to help.

I handed in my resignation with immediate effect.

What Will You Lay On The Altar?

There's this thing about divine purpose that is inescapable: it requires sacrifice. After pressing send on that resignation email with the event due to launch the next night, I went home and sat on my bed, wondering what I was going to do now. I didn't even have the resources it took to make this series of events a reality. All I had was this knowing that this was what I was supposed to do, and I was finally, FINALLY, ready to listen, ready to trust, ready to believe.

I looked over one of my favourite quotes and sighed:

"Until one is committed, there is hesitancy, the chance to draw back, always ineffectiveness. Concerning all acts of initiative (and creation), there is one elementary truth, the ignorance of which kills countless ideas and splendid plans. That the moment one definitely commits oneself, then providence moves, too. All sorts of things occur to help one that would never otherwise have occurred." – William H. Murray.

I looked up and told Providence — God — only one thing: "Your move."

The rest of this story tears me up every single time because it's still unbelievable to me, and I lived it! My phone rang, moments after, and it was a person calling to say that their company had agreed to be a small cash sponsor of my events. The meeting had just ended, and the man wanted me to know so that the launch wouldn't happen without their involvement. After profusely thanking him and hanging up the phone, tears beginning to stream from my eyes. I said to this Providence: "Okay, fine, point received, even if that's not going to be quite enough to cover all that's ahead. You're clearly asking me to trust, so I will."

The next day was my last day at my regular job and the first night of my events. I went in, packed up my things, spoke to my boss and her boss (both of whom I loved and respected dearly), and felt the haze of tears many times. After lunch, as I cleared my desk, I picked up the picture frame which held the photo of my son, my why.

"Am I doing the right thing?" I wondered, but only for a second, as the absolute will of divine Guidance pushed back with a resounding "YES!" [A quick note to you, my reader: any use I make of a capital "G" for Guidance refers to what I believe is Guidance from God/ being divinely guided.]

I could feel all the way to my bones that this was what it was like to be divinely guided by something beyond me, something that knew all that was ahead — the comfort of "maktub" amid despair. So, I aligned with it. And the strength of belief that powered into me was instantly matched as my phone rang once again.

This time, it was a call from another agency with a decision that raises goosebumps to this day: to be the title sponsor of my entire series of events, with immediate effect.

I launched my series that night with a greater understanding than I had had in all of my adult years. It was even more meaningful to have the full support of my family, with my brother both present and proud at the launch.

We will be divinely cared for if we are willing to sacrifice the good for the great, the sensible for the calling, the ease for the purpose. It may not happen right away, or even in our timing, because there's another Clock in play that we can't always perceive… but we can tune into it through the act of trust.

Can You Hear The Song's Call?

To say these events were superbly successful requires you to understand the intention behind them and my metrics for success. They weren't massively populated — they competed with the parties of the carnival season — but they were incredibly revealing. For me, they were a crash-course in connections between the creative industries. A system began to form within my mind for all that could come together, perhaps even on a national level. I felt more fired up on purpose than I had in such a long time.

As the eight weeks of events ended, I itched for more projects to create such connections and provide more opportunities. I had determined that I would never allow myself to be employed by another company. Having seen the power wielded over my entire career for having a heart and putting action behind it, I didn't want to put myself in such a position again. I wanted only to render myself into service, and this became my mission.

A few potential projects popped up, but none

seemed to find their way to the finish line of a handshake or contractual commitment. The increasing barrenness of my bank account began to weigh on me once again, and I wondered what I was meant to do next and if I had missed the signal. I was thirty-years-old, with a six-year-old son [my village in hand], yet with no sense of my future financial security. It was disconcerting to have jumped off a cliff with all of the excitement of an adventure with *God,* only to then find myself drifting on that vast ocean without any indication of what was to come.

Just as I could only see my way through one more month of living expenses, I got an unexpected call from the same state agency in the creative industries to which I had submitted my resume while doing my first series of events. I had moved on from that opportunity because I had never received a call back after the interview, and around six months had passed. The man in charge of the music arm wanted to know if I was still available for the position and if I could come in to chat.

It was a dilemma. I had just decided that I would never work for another company again because of the risk of being ordered away from my purpose, but here was someone dangling not only the security of a steady salary, but an influential position in an industry that I desperately wanted to help. I was overflowing with ideas but had no outlet, and they had an outlet for those very ideas.

I decided to do what came easiest for me: to make it very, very difficult for him to want to hire me. I spoke openly about how I worked and what I believed in, the integrity I needed to be a part of the process, and the methodology for accountability. I talked about my company on the side [wasn't making that mistake twice] and everything else that I thought would scare this offer away. I figured that only *God* would allow it to remain on the table with all of the ridiculous verbal vomit of my truth and my need to live it.

Instead, the man who would become my boss for the next few years found my truth to be refreshing and reasonable and asked how soon I could start.

I'm convinced God has a ridiculous sense of humour. I shook my head when I signed that contract, and then I allowed myself to feel all of the hope in the world. Perhaps I could make a difference. Perhaps this was the opportunity to make a lasting contribution to an industry I loved beyond expression. Perhaps this had all been for a meaning greater than I could ever imagine.

And, perhaps, I wasn't all that rejected by God after

all.

The Point Of Renewal

I would be lying if I said that this particular career path wasn't a difficult one, and anyone who has ever been involved in politics — even on the fringes — would tell you the same. Within the first year of me being there, I got a full dose of the worst and best parts of people's agendas, and the greatest challenge was proving in material terms how significant the work of the creative industries was for national development. It didn't matter which government was in charge or who was leading our charge — the battles, the war, remained.

Each one of my fellow General Managers (one for film, one for fashion, and me for music) faced that challenge repeatedly, and we fought battles on behalf of stakeholders that they would never know of and, perhaps, never understand. We were the bridge between the industry and the government, and as such, we were, at times, trampled upon by both sides without remorse. Still, we each fought valiantly in our own ways, as did most of those on the boards and those employed, and that by itself is an experience that I cherish.

However, there was an expiry date in play that I didn't see coming at the time. The season for those "pass-the-time" careers was over, but the season for "pass-the-time" relationships was also closing more quickly than I had expected.

The make-or-break arrived when I came out of a connection in which I had profoundly disappointed myself — and I mean that quite literally. It had lasted around six months, and during that time, I found that the value systems we each had seemed to be butting heads more and more often. Coming down to the end, we had a trip planned together, and before leaving for it, I spoke to one of my girlfriends once again about navigating this minefield I felt within me. She gave me a powerful suggestion: "Why not just let everything go that weekend? Don't comment on anything, don't ask for anything, keep smiling, and observe what he decides to do."

The point was to see who he was, especially if he didn't have to keep who I was in mind. I thought it was a genius suggestion for my research, and it was. That entire weekend passed by beautifully, with him saying and doing all sorts of things that poked at my values and sense of self-worth, while I grinned and took it all with openness. I kept that smile plastered on while I faced the reality of seeing someone be who they truly were — and realising that this person wasn't what I wanted in a partner, or in love.

When he dropped me off at the airport to head back home, however, he said the words that crushed my entire being: "This was the best weekend ever with you!" Can you imagine it? I had not been any of who I was, while allowing him to be all that he was, and he had had an entirely different experience of the same weekend. He hadn't even noticed that I hadn't been me. He had only basked in how happy he felt to finally be him — and there was absolutely nothing wrong with that [him being himself].

The relationship ended shortly after, but the lesson kept churning in the back of my mind. What was I missing in all of my experiments? What was the piece that I couldn't fit into this puzzle I had created? For the next month or two, I brooded over my series of experiments from the last four years and kept trying to connect the dots in the data. Then, I opened myself to Guidance, the divine intuition that sparks all the answers, and I asked for help.

In an instant, I saw myself in what I could only describe as a sort of imaginary vision. I was standing outside a cave in the brightest, warmest sunshine, with birds chirping all around me and water gurgling from the nearby stream.

It felt peaceful and happy here, and I wanted to share it with this particular ex, but then I saw him — he was deep in that dark cave, relaxing in a corner with his legs outstretched and crossed. The darkness only represented the contrast between the comforts of my environment and his. He was just as much at peace, enjoying the coolness of the cave and the markings on the walls.

I entered in search of him, and when I found him, I panicked that he seemed stuck in that dark cave. I ran back out and gathered as much light as my hands could carry, and then I rushed back into the cave to show him all that he was missing outside. When I shoved all the light straight into his face, he shouted out in pain and blocked his eyes, aggrieved by my insensitivity to what his eyes were used to in his sensory experience of life.

The vision ended there, and it was then that I understood it. It was like being curled up sleeping in a dark bedroom, and having someone sweep in and switch on all the brightest lights, with no regard for the comfort of your sleep. It's excruciatingly annoying and even painful. Even more than that, it doesn't make you love the light or the person who has switched it on — only despise it, and maybe even the person.

For the entire period of my "pass-the-time"

experimentation in relationships, ultimately, that is what I had been doing. I had shoved my value system into the faces of others or tried to abide in their environments, with no regard for a simple fact: we are not all meant to live in the same places, nor the same ways.

My experiment had been doomed to fail since the start because I had been so focused on wanting people to accept and adapt to who I was that I hadn't made room for who they were and what they believed. In wanting — no, needing — so desperately to never lose the remnants of myself that I had begun to find once again, I had set a standard that was the rarest to find: a connection in which one person being herself didn't block the other from actualising who he was here to be, but instead, those two beings enhanced each other's becoming. As I looked back on the various souls I had connected with, and the many times this lesson had tried to reach me, I shook my head at my insistence on learning this the hard and long way.

I then did the one thing I felt I could do: I decided to simply focus on finding, knowing, and being who I was, and left the thoughts of lifelong love, acceptance, and rising together to those who had found a way to do it. I knew the price of not being or becoming who I was, and after understanding that this price existed for each person, I could no longer allow another connection that would compromise this essence in them or me.

I consciously ended my experiment when I understood what this twisted journey had tried to teach me, and as I did, another vision appeared from the back of my mind. It rolled gently over my consciousness and transported me to another world, where I came face-to-face with a blue-haired, sixteen-year-old girl on a planet called Mira.

Her name was Yara. She told me that because I had opened myself to the lessons of light and darkness, finally accepting the duality of existence to be less about right or wrong and more a state of being, I was ready for what was next. She believed I had new eyes, and she relished using them to show me her life. As for "what was next," it was simple (though only for her): she wanted me to tell her story.

PART THREE

CLIMBING YOUR MOUNTAIN AND MAKING YOUR MARK

CHAPTER SEVEN

GAINING CONFIDENCE

It was the most enchanting, soothing, and exhilarating sound you'd ever heard. You didn't quite understand how it had happened, but the fact that you could perceive your mountain once again filled you with a sense of purpose and even belonging.

It didn't matter that you had been the one to block out the song when you numbed yourself to the pain of the valley. At the time, you believed all the mountains had betrayed you, so desensitising yourself to the shock and pain had felt like your only defence. It had never occurred to you, not until the moment the song enveloped your soul once more, that you had pushed away the only reason that the journey had mattered: the pull of your calling.

You had set out from your birth mountain in search of the place from which the song came. You had left because to stay felt like a denial and betrayal of the person you knew you were meant to become. Yet, when your birth mountain ring was stolen upon entry into the valley, you had allowed it to destroy all sense of hope from the pull of the song. So many horrific events had happened since then that the stolen ring seemed like the complaint of a toddler whose toy was taken away.

As you pondered on this, you realised that this was absolute proof of the strength you had gained, visible in your lean and muscular reflection. As your mountain's call lingered in your ears, you could feel it affecting your sense of balance and direction. Your head and body tilted as if perceiving the pull of the next step, and you felt utterly imbalanced until you began to place one foot in front of the other and head towards it.

Each step you took eased the dewy dizziness of your surrender, and as sights and sounds began to change, you knew you were no longer locked into your circle. Instead, you were well on your way, with energy that felt very similar to when you'd first set off, but layered with wisdom, insight, and strength from your experiences that you were just beginning to process.

You saw a dip in the ground and knew it was a stumbling risk. You stepped around it. You saw a jagged root that typically would have tripped you up, but instead, you took a little leap. It didn't always work out well, though — you quite literally came face-to-face with a massive branch after that little leap. It knocked you over for a second, but this time, you laughed and reminded yourself to look at more than just the ground when you were walking.

And so, as you straightened your back and then your neck, you saw more of what was ahead and took better steps. You even twisted around now and then to make sure nothing was stalking you in the dark foliage that surrounded the strange path. As you improved your strides, your confidence and your awareness grew, and the unfamiliar places in the valley didn't seem quite as terrifying. There was beauty there that you had been too consumed to recognise, but now it filled your eyes and softened your heart.

Then, without notice, the fog broke all around you, rapidly pulling back its billows into the earth. Before you, the most majestic mountain you had ever seen now stood, glistening with vapour and bursting with green life. But… it was also the steepest, tallest, and most terrifying formation you'd ever beheld.

"I have no idea how I'm going to climb this mountain," your thoughts whispered, "so then, why do I feel so alive?"

To Feel Underwhelmed Is A Superpower

It's a strange thing to say, I know; it's the opposite of feeling alive, but I have found that the path to an exhilarating experience of life begins with pruning the dead and decaying parts within us. The very thought of feeling underwhelmed seems like one of the worst possible realities to exist. Despite this, many people are very much underwhelmed by their current lives, except that they don't know that they are. Or, at least, I didn't. And no one can address an illness without first identifying or defining its symptoms.

For me, there was a strange, restless energy always present, even if I was out with friends or spending time with family, but I couldn't quite put my finger on what — if anything — was wrong. It was like a faint ringing in my ears that I tried to drown out with the noise of a full (not fulfilling) life. At times, I found myself extra snappy or on-edge, and it was difficult to maintain a lasting sense of happiness or joy.

I had moments, yes, but then it all slipped away and, when it was quiet enough — too quiet — that faint ringing began again.

So, to counter it, I continued to fill my life with all sorts of activities: fitness plans, fun with friends, quality time with loved ones, hobbies and, above all else, professional pursuits. I went after goals, ticked off travel destinations, and just generally lived a seemingly fulfilled life.

I've had friends express that their symptoms showed up in different ways to mine. They were the ones who, apart from doing the minimum to keep a regular salary coming in, were the couch potatoes. To clock-out of the listlessness of work was to clock-in to the fun of binging on whatever filled the time and took up the rest of their energy. Then, they went to sleep and got up the next day to do it all over again.

The problem wasn't so much what we were choosing to do or not do, but the fact that we couldn't identify what our symptoms meant. Something was very, very wrong. And what was wrong was that we were underwhelmed. It didn't seem to matter if we were at the top of the best global entities in the world or the bottom of a bottle in a bar. This elusive dissatisfaction remained the thread that tied us all, the plague that infected our existence, and we did not know it!

To know it, however, is to make the first step towards having the power to change it.

So, the magic of the underwhelming is this: **the minute you feel it, you can no longer deny the truth of what your life has become, and you are irresistibly compelled to change it.** To feel the magic of the underwhelming is to experience the birthing of purpose. Even if you don't yet know what you're supposed to do or how to do it, you know that you need to change and that your life will never be the same.

When Yara, my blue-haired girl, decided to "show" me her story so I could write it, I had just identified that this underwhelmed undertone existed within me. Whether it was due to my pass-the-time experiments in love and careers, or my realisation of the missing pieces of alignment in my hypotheses, I came face-to-face with how filled-yet-unfulfilling my life had become. Yara, alongside my creative pursuits, birthed a renewed sense of purpose that required an insatiable appetite for both risk and growth. Our connection is one I hope to explain fully one day, but above all else, she represented the appearance of my mountain. Yara made me feel alive!

The problem? While having journaled and written

for my studies/professions in the past, and although fantasy/ sci-fi was my favourite genre in the books and movies I consumed, I had never been a fiction writer. I also did not know a single thing about how to write a book, much less one that was fantastical, and when I understood that Yara was only sixteen years old, I knew I was, for the most part, targeting her fellow young adults. This meant needing to tap back into sixteen-year-old me while staying in touch with the sixteen-year-olds of the present, and writing from a place they would easily understand.

Can I also add in the fact that *none* of this felt remotely connected to me becoming a research scientist one day? And granted, I was the General Manager of a state agency in the music industry, which technically was not in line with that either. So, if anything, I would have thought that my extracurricular goals should carry me closer to my childhood dreams, not further away. Being a GM was an intense weight on my shoulders without adding the most random fictional books to my pursuits.

Oh, and how can I forget: Yara didn't just want to be a book. She wanted to be a trilogy, and a movie, and a whole world to explore. Talk about demanding! I reached out to one of my BFFs and told him about her craziness and the pull that

I felt to this girl's otherworldly story. My exhilaration showed. His response was simple yet powerful: write it!

Cracking Open My Inner-World Door

Easier said than done.

I'd love to pretend that an incredible wave of enthusiasm and purpose then crashed through me and swept all of my doubts away, allowing me to birth the books with one giant push… but, this isn't that kind of fairytale (which, *by now*, you should know).

Instead, Queen Hem-and-Haw over here groaned and grunted about how exceedingly silly she would seem if she randomly wrote storybooks after spending all of her life in pursuit of "professional" careers that were more "rational." [Let me not add further to that "silliness" by continuing to talk about myself in the third person.] To become not just a public-facing writer, but the kind who would share my imaginary worlds with their imaginary friends, was the bane of my projected existence.

I had grown accustomed to being the one who contributed to the business of creatives, rather than letting myself be one. I had also grown accustomed to applying — and many times, misapplying — the scientific method to life. While the process of fantastical writing had structure, the content had to be sourced from an eerily naked place within me.

I decided that I needed to experience the uncomfortable exposure I felt at the thought of sharing my personal thoughts in a public way. It wouldn't be quite the same as fiction, but if I could openly post my theories on life to my social media, and face how damning it felt to do so, maybe I could build up the courage one day to share my insane inner worlds.

Thus, my "sharing era" began: an intentionally shared set of blog posts over a two-year period on whatever I felt led to write. From intense thought pieces to lighter poetry to the connecting points behind experiences, I navigated a new world that likely shocked those who partook in the before-and-after of my posts. Each one came with that irk inside as I pressed the button to expose more of me, and as I began to trace the root of the irk, I found it planted in the soils of fear.

Some fears were reasonable, and they remain so even as I type this. One of my most prominent fears was this: how can I share a theory or lesson I've learnt about life when I'm still growing, and my views may change? This one was rooted in my dogmatic Christian days when I had been determined to convert everyone I knew; yet, soon after reaching adulthood, I had rejected the very thing I shouted about from the mountaintops.

How could anyone take anything I had to say seriously after that? Why should they? Even worse, what if I led someone down a path that was either wrong, or wrong for them, and they ended up getting hurt because they trusted in my words? The responsibility behind that fear weighed heavily on me, as there would be times I'd advance so quickly in a particular area that I would feel sick to my stomach seeing something I had written not too long before.

What was my recourse? Should I have deleted posts like that? Is anything ever really "deleted" in the online space? I'm sure we've all seen how capable tabloids are of digging up decades-old posts made by prominent politicians, for example, when they were the idiotic [read: youthful] versions of themselves. Cancel culture is real; shame culture is real. We don't make space for people to evolve into better versions of themselves because we're usually too busy chastising them for all that they haven't yet been (even if their evolution is in progress).

And I couldn't blame those chastisers because I was busy blaming myself. How could I account for the choices and views of Past-Me when Present-Me felt far removed from her? What then did that mean for Future-Me's view of who I was today? Should anyone ever share anything until they were on their dying beds with little room for massive change? With life already being a chaotic mess to work through for most people, should adding more chaos be a priority? There was no easy answer to any of these, and there still isn't, but for anyone who struggles with this, I'll pause here and tell you my three anchors:

1. **I try my best to never speak for Future-Me.** I've lived with myself for long enough to know that I am hellbent on self-improvement and personal development. I can never sit still if there is a chance to grow, and I abhor the very notion of stagnancy. I know I'm going to grow, and this means I won't be who I am today or who I was yesterday in some really significant ways.
2. **I try my best to honour Past-Me's choices because she did the best she could.** Let's be real here: there's a tonne of crap that I once felt that

I needed to be horribly ashamed of, forever. I paid my undue dues, beating myself up for not knowing things I didn't know, or for feeling things I believed I shouldn't have felt, and there was *no one* better at pounding me than me. I am *done* with that crap. DONE. This is my story, with a few of the parts expressed in this book, and I will own all of it and love me all the way to my healing.

3. **I refuse, under any circumstances, to be held captive by a past or future version of me.** There were so many times that I held myself back from being or doing something based either on the cage my past-self had put me in or the person my future-self was pressuring me to be. I had neglected to honour my present, and so much of the joy that could be found within it, by focusing on everything else but what was in front of me at the moment. We lose so much from today by regretting yesterday and worrying about tomorrow. I can only give my all in the here and now, and by doing this, I am honouring the sacredness of the time gifted to me.

As to the unreasonable fears that plagued me in sharing my musings, you probably know a few of them well: what would people think; what if I'm coming across as overbearing; what if people don't like what I have to say; what if it helps no one, *ever*; what if someone uses my personal thoughts against me, etc. See what those all have in common? They were *all* about everyone else.

And they weren't unfounded fears. I had an acquaintance come up to me once, almost offended that I had been posting such long captions under some of my photos, saying something like, "Every time I see something like that from you now, I just shake my head and groan, because there you go again. Don't you know that's not what social media is for? People ain't trying to read all that!"

Was he correct? In many ways, he probably was, but it didn't have anything to do with my initial intention: getting myself used to opening up and sharing, and being able to take the backlash whenever and however it came, without losing sight of my mission. Add in the audacity of anyone trying to dictate what you should and shouldn't do on your social media outlets, and I became a professional cage-breaker. If I weren't allowing Past-and-Future-Me to put me in their cages, then no one else would ever be allowed to put me in theirs.

So, my response to him? "My social media is my space. If you don't like what's there, you can just unfollow."

It was suddenly so simple, so very, very simple. I was putting out a beacon to my people, my tribe, those who would walk with me and dine with me in the ethos of our existence. If someone didn't resonate with what I had to share, then my share wasn't *for* them. It wasn't offensive, not even remotely; it just was what it was.

And, as my strength in sharing from a deeper place grew, I began to map out Yara's story while beginning my online courses and studies on how to write her fantastical trilogy.

Love Enters, Stage Left

You never see it coming, do you? I know everyone who's found that "something" with their "someone" always says that, but let me tell you: left-field is real!

My long-term boyfriend and I met maybe thirteen years before we entered into anything romantic, and we weren't even close friends during that time. My impression of him was the same as everyone who knew him: he's such a cool, chill guy! He was a rock to those in his circle, and the friend you'd reach out to for a connection or reference for practically anything. His recommendation, and very existence, was one you could trust, and all of our limited interactions over the years oozed with that calm knowing.

Things changed when we were brought together for the birthday of a mutual friend, and upon engaging in a discussion about the business of the music industry, I found that the depths of his views on the topic confounded me. He was so much more than he had ever let on, and the way he held back seemed intentional: he was far more interested in getting to know you than in being known. I came away from the interaction thinking, "this guy is definitely going to be one of my close friends," and when he messaged the next day, I knew it had been a mutually intriguing experience.

Still, I didn't know *God* was setting me up at the time. I had merely been craving the kinds of minds that could deep dive with me across varied topics and perspectives because let's not forget: I was done with companionship. I knew it was impossible to find a connection in which two souls could both be themselves and fulfil their purposes, so even with the chemistry, I didn't let myself go there. I had given up trying to find that person, through my experiments or otherwise, and I assumed that, if anything at all, I would spend my life in casual engagements with no significant future.

Yet, it appears that God can only step in when we give up trying to be God on our own behalf. We get so busy holding on to the reins of our lives that we forget we can't see what's coming. Maybe, at some point, it only makes sense to hand them over to Someone who can.

But I digress.

A month after our first "divine set-up," following an unexpected eight-hour-straight conversation that crossed topics and worlds and the very ethos of us both, I knew this was no joke. It was a little while after that, on our first official date, that I began to understand our connection. I hadn't shared Yara's story with anyone outside of that one BFF at the time, and I wouldn't have risked doing so because of how ridiculous the pursuit still felt within me. I needed all the encouragement I could get, and explaining that a random blue-haired girl had appeared from another world in a sort of vision and asked me to tell her story was the kind of crazy I figured no one needed to know.

At the end of this date, however, as we were sitting in the car, still unable to stop sharing, it all came rushing out — not how the story came to me, but what the story was. In the back of my mind, my logical side was screaming, "Are you crazy?! We don't even know this guy well enough to do that!" but there I was, walking along the path to openness with a whole trail of verbal spews behind me.

He listened, seemingly engaged, until I concluded the entire trilogy plot as Yara had told me, word-for-word. Then, after a few moments of silence, he said the most unexpected and unforgettable thing: "That did not come from you."

"What do you mean?" I pressed.

"That had to have come from some place beyond you. You have to write it…"

He knew, without me saying, that the connection I had felt to Yara and her story was from another realm. It hadn't been me trying to make up a story so I could become a fantastical author. It was me, coming face-to-face with an existential crisis in the form of this teenage alien-girl.

No one had ever seen me, felt me, in such a profound way before that point. Every ounce of my embarrassment and self-consciousness about this path melted away in his presence. He believed not only in the story, but in my ability to tell it, with a seriousness that felt like he could see right into my soul.

And just like that, sitting in the car with him, opening

up and sharing my vulnerable side felt more like a gift from God than a pressured choice. A passing thought flittered through my mind: "Looks like you're both being yourselves..."

Love Calls You Out

And so, they lived happily ever after...

Yeah, right!

Again, this isn't a fairytale. I'd liken it more to a hero's journey in which the villain was also the hero — on steroids! We can be our own worst enemies in ways that continue to baffle me, yet guess who defaulted into that mode the minute something incredible came along? **raises hand while my ego scrambles to put it back down**

We weren't perfect; no one is. He had a frightening view on life that left me disconcerted for the first year of our relationship. It revealed itself within the first few months as I did my usual in an attempt to understand who I was dealing with — personality tests, questionnaires, and lots of discussions about value systems and guidelines.

My default view was still quite simple, and I think this analogy explains it best: if we're going to build a house together, then we both need to contribute to the architectural design. Who wants windows where and how many stories high and the use of each room and should there be a garden… it's a two-person job. So, with this in mind, I'd ask him about his desires for the "house" and the things he knew he wouldn't want in it. I'd explain the things I'd want and ask for his take on them so we could ensure there was enough common ground upon which to build.

His response, *every time*, was the most annoying words, despite my agreement with the concept (when not coming out of his mouth): "Follow your Guidance. That's all I want, nothing more, nothing less."

"Umm, yeah, I get that, but how do you feel about me doing x, y, z where other guys are concerned, or exes are concerned?"

"Just follow your Guidance. I'm good with whatever you feel led to do. No tricks; no games; no consequences. I'm here for all of it."

What-the-actual-#$%&?!!!

As far as I was concerned, this *had* to be some kind of trick or game! Who doesn't have preferences and desires and ways they want to be treated in love and respect?!

His response? "I don't believe in having those kinds

of desires. I want you to be all you came here to be, and I want the same for me. As long as you're tuning into that, and not doing things from a place of vice, for example, I'm good — I really, *really* am. I just want to see you soar."

Now, folks, I am well aware that this was EXACTLY what I wanted, but also believed I would NEVER find in another human being — EVER. Still, even with its appearance, your girl wasn't about to buy that crap wholesale! If it were *really* true, and not too-good-to-be-true (as it had been with everyone else), then… what had I done to deserve such a blessing in my life? I had messed up in all sorts of ways, made the most mistakes ever, and I still didn't have a complete handle on who I was becoming. This is one of the destructive effects of shame: it makes us believe our mistakes define us and that we don't deserve to have the most magnanimous dreams come true.

And yes, I wanted a connection where both people could be who they were and do what they were here to do, but, it turns out, my relationship retort was differently sourced. The *jaded* reason I desperately wanted him to be himself fully and never, *ever*, do anything FOR me (due to a desire I expressed or a way I loved being treated) was this: I knew that all masks cracked, as is the destiny of masks, so I wanted to save myself the catastrophic pain of believing I had found my impossible dream, and it all turning out to be a lie. My self-defence system activated, rejecting anything that he wanted to contribute to my life for fear that it would break.

It didn't take him very long to perceive my fears or to call me out on them. He identified two things that I did, habitually, when faced with the risk of projected pain: I either ran away, or I quickly patched up my feelings rather than dealing with them — or, most of the time, both. I admitted to facing those challenges, and then, despite my fears, I opened up about a lot of what I'd been through and how that had made me very capable of piling everything under the rug. I also admitted to not having a clue about how to deal with the intense emotions from those experiences, and how I worried about my ability to write Yara's story when I couldn't even emotionally express mine.

Without being asked, and without any expectation, I soon received a gifted Kindle book in my inbox (as was his nature), called Emotional Agility by Susan David, PhD.

Prior to reading that book, I viewed emotions as potential inconveniences. They could mess up an average day, and they could make something normal seem far more incredible than it was — and then, the joke would be on you. They were these annoying amplifiers that turned everything up or down at will, and without notice, and I just preferred that they stay in their corner, and I stay in mine.

This isn't to say that I didn't enjoy a good laugh or even a good cry… while laughing, but the rest of it felt risky and unavoidable, so I would just tolerate the existence of emotions (or have a full-blown tantrum) and wait for them to dissipate once again. The problem with this is simple: **you can't touch anyone if you're out of touch.** And while the intention of attaining emotional agility should be more about you becoming your best version rather than anything else, a part of your best version has to do with relating to the world. It matters. All of it matters.

While I can't begin to get into the range of issues that this book addressed within me, there's one that I'll share for this discussion. Dr Susan David introduced a concept called "hooks," and suggested that there are four common ones that happen when "people who are hooked into a particular way of thinking or behaving are not really paying attention to the world as it is." Of all the hooks she spoke about, there was one in particular that I engaged in more than I care to admit, called "Monkey-mindedness."

Have you ever fallen out with a friend or co-worker and found yourself deep in a mock conversation of all the things you're going to say, then what they're going to say, and then how you're going to respond (ad infinitum)? David argues that by the time you're done with this, you're completely worn out from the intense but *fictional* confrontation that took place, and that we do this because "when we're in monkey-mind mode, it's easy to start "awfulising" — imagining worst-case scenarios or making too much of a minor problem." In a sense, it's when we allow our thoughts to swing from thing to thing, back and forth, just like a monkey does between trees, except it's all in the service of our "imaginary dramas."

This was all very hit-home-why-don't-ya to me, but it was another line in this section that seeded a different thought.

David said, "Monkey mind is obsessed with the push of the past ("I just can't forgive what he did") and the pull of the future ("I can't wait to quit and give my manager a piece of my mind"). It's also often filled with bossy, judgmental inner language, words like "must" and "can't" and "should" ("I must lose weight," "I can't fail," "I shouldn't feel this way"). Monkey mind takes you out of the moment and out of what is best for your life."

Did you read all of that? Because I didn't. At that moment, I couldn't get past the "push of the past" and her hard-hitting example: "I just can't forgive what he did."

To Forgive He Who Wanted You Dead

I should mention that the day my boyfriend sent me this book on Kindle was the day before the tenth anniversary of my ex's attempt to kill me. In a sense, I entered that day with the worded power of the very thing that would bring me healing. In the couple of months that followed, as I delved deeply into every bit of that book, I kept coming back to that point of ponderance: was I stuck in the past?

On the surface, I certainly wasn't. My boyfriend had made the bold move of asking me to live together, and we had found a house in a quiet neighbourhood where we could begin building our new lives. I was a couple of years into my

GM job while learning about writing fiction on the side, my son was eight and great (at *everything*), and all else progressed at a reasonable pace. Nothing was really wrong-wrong, but within me, I knew I hadn't begun to face my darkest demons.

It occurred to me, shortly after reading the book, that I wanted to fully commit myself to the path of understanding the emotions within me, past and present. I felt like I had uncovered a secret beneath the inconvenience of feelings, and that if I could get past the discomfort and pain they caused, I'd find a well of powerful data, like breadcrumbs for the path ahead. Finding the trail was easy — I just had to look at what was screaming out.

With my ex, it was the numbness that screamed out. I tried hard not to think too much about it, except around the anniversary (when the darker thoughts would creep in). I would wipe them all away as quickly as they appeared, refusing to let myself feel through any of it. I had decided it would be the most horrifying and debilitating experience in the entire world, and I was hooked on that narrative for a whole decade.

Now, with my newfound strength, I turned inward. Much to my surprise, I found that I was stronger than I had thought. I didn't break; I didn't find myself rocking in a corner. If I had, there would have been nothing wrong with that either. However, over the ten years that had passed, I had begun to build up little pieces of myself from my brokenness. I had found peace in understanding my missteps, and comfort in seeing the extent of my compassion.

The best part of all? I found not an ounce of the hate left towards him in my entire being. Not. A. Single. Ounce. All I felt, instead, was a release in that it was time to forgive him, and a hope that he had done the work to recover and then forgiven himself.

The Point Of Alignment

Within a month of this freeing discovery, I felt led one day to message this ex and let him know that I no longer held any hate in my heart. Most people (in their supposed right minds) would think this kind of Guidance is both crazy of me and more than he deserved. I am not most people. I believed, instead, that the very best-case scenario that could ever take place was for a man like him to get better, to overcome his demons, to forgive himself, and to make a purposeful contribution to the world thereafter, even if only by the way he lived.

It struck me on the day I wrote to him that if I died that very day, I would have never released him from the burden I knew he bore, and I didn't want to ever leave anyone with burdens. And so, while he and I may never be close again, I gave him my forgiveness and requested that he also forgive himself.

Out of an abundance of care, given the sensitive nature of this topic, I will leave the details of the rest of the exchange private. Still, I will say this much: it was one of the most important conversations I had that year, for his sake and, in a liberating way, for mine. Still, while forgiveness is undoubtedly a gift we can give ourselves and others, the reaching-out part is not a path I recommend for everyone; it could be dangerous in all the obvious ways. I followed my Guidance from God there, and each person should do the same.

God's Guidance will always lead you exactly where you're supposed to go, even when it's to the most unlikely of places. Following Guidance isn't reserved for just things like big career or relationship decisions. It spans everything, from the significant to the seemingly insignificant, because what it's really about is your ability to do three powerful things:

1. Tune-in
2. Listen
3. Follow

Alignment — following your Guidance — is the same as training the muscles in your body to push heavy weights or stretching them into complex yoga positions or running ten-kilometre races: you have to commit to a regular, progressive practice.

But, BIG but, what represents alignment for one person may be misalignment for you. The steps cannot be patterned or replicated, and there isn't a checklist you can follow. You have to find it for yourself, within yourself, and be bold enough to trust whatever is being asked of you… even amid grave uncertainty.

CHAPTER EIGHT

WIELDING UNCERTAINTY

"Where should I start this climb?" you wondered as you walked along the base of the gigantic mountain. You had hoped to find an easier way to start your ascent, but the further you strode, the less inviting the climb seemed.

Something within you had suggested that where you'd first arrived at your mountain was where you should begin, but it seemed irrational to not check for a better path first. This checking had only served to inject a bit of doubt, and soon your enthusiasm began to plummet. It was then that you remembered the mountain's song, always present now in the back of your mind, and you closed your eyes to better hear its soothing flow. As it reminded you of why you were there, you began your pacing once again, this time allowing the incrementally small changes in volume to pull you closer to its source.

These almost imperceptible variations carried you right back to where you had first seen your mountain, and now as you surveyed it, you noticed something strange along the rock wall. There was a slight wind coming through the vines at the bottom of the steep face. You walked up to it, the song now at the loudest it had ever been, and pulled hard at the vines, tearing them away to find strange markings and small crevices. They weren't large enough for anything other than toes and fingers — precisely what you needed to scale the rock wall.

However, it would be a free climb and a dangerous one at that, as it would be a while before you'd get to the ledge where the trees began. Perhaps then the climb would level off, although by now, you knew better than to hope for anything. It would always be whatever it was, and you had finally learnt enough to know one thing: you'd grow stronger while learning how to handle it, and you would be able to handle it.

And so, with a deep breath and a renewed sense of clarity, you grabbed on and pulled yourself up, eyes fixed on the ledge far above.

The Imperceptible Change

On the morning of the day I resigned from my GM position at the state agency, I didn't know that it was going to be my resignation day. I had suspected it was coming: I could feel the hints of changes within me, editing my direction and pulling me gently towards this result, but the day it happened began just like any other day.

I got up, got dressed, and put on my percolator (oh, for the love of coffee), and as I waited with my mug in hand, I felt the suddenness of knowing, and the immediacy of this guided request. I didn't understand why at the time, but I was being asked to leave my job which I loved, despite the expected politics involved, and put all of my energy into —

"You can't be serious! You want me to leave to write this blue-haired Yara's story?! *Why*? I can do both!" I retorted. It was the most ridiculous request I ever had made of me by Guidance, to leave a great job with a purposeful mission — that also paid my bills — to do something that was not only risky but wholly, nakedly creative.

Want to know what made it worse? I didn't even have a plan in place. It had been almost two years since Yara had appeared, and I had only finished her synopsis [read: a

17,000-word mini-book] a few months before. I had also just completed my very first draft of the first chapter of the book.

Oh, and I didn't have a nest egg.

If anyone came to me for advice with this, I would tell them to do the wise thing: "You want to jump off a cliff? Sure! Just make sure you have a safety net in place. Ain't nothing wrong with a little backup plan!"

I got lost in my thoughts on the way to work. Even when I walked into my office and sat down behind my desk, I wasn't there. I felt torn and rather miserable, because unlike the time I had resigned with immediate effect, right there, right then, there was nothing *wrong* with my job. Things were slowly progressing despite the tough economic climate. Fascinating projects were underway, and to me, they felt like my babies. Although I had known for a few months that I would be asked at some point to pass on the baton to another incredible soul, I hadn't thought it would be so soon.

Let's not even talk about how I felt when I considered having to explain to my boyfriend, and the rest of my family, that I had thrown away an excellent gig for an unknown outcome. I searched within myself for another path, a different way. I considered giving myself one more year to be sure about this, and even commended myself on that solid rational.

Then, I typed my resignation notice and pressed send.

The Undeniable Truth

Here's the thing about **Guidance: it is a light that only you can see, and only you can follow.** It's not up to anyone else, because only you can decide to listen. You can't expect to get validation from a single soul outside of yourself, because it is not for them to see or know — only you, and you alone.

However, it doesn't have to be a lonely experience, because here's the other thing: **people who know what it is to be guided, and who follow that light even to the most unlikely of places, are far more likely to understand and encourage you to do the same. Even more than that, they are far more likely to redirect you to yourself when you come sniffing around for that external validation you *don't* need.**

Note those people! Make a list and check it twice because those are your people, your tribe, the ones who are connected to Divinity, to God. I'm not talking about your "yes people," who just agree with whatever you have to say, nor am I saying that those who ask questions to understand the root of your intentions aren't a part of this group. I am speaking about those who ultimately encourage you to follow *God's* Guidance — not theirs — in the end.

I had learnt enough along my journey to know that any other version of me approaching my resignation would be me resisting the sacred call. Still, I was a bit mortified when I contacted my boyfriend to say, "Hi… Sooooooooo, I just resigned."

When I did, however, who he was, who he is, showed as it always does. I explained what I had felt, and the pull to do it, and no matter what must have run through his head from a human place, his response was what it had always been: follow your Guidance and trust the process. I thank God for his anchor every single day, I kid you not.

This didn't stop me from descending into a pit of fear and guilt, though. Was I *really* leaving my professional, high-end job to go and write storybooks? This view was also shared by a few people in my life who wrote and called and visited me (and even my closest friends) to ask, "Are you crazy?! Who leaves such a top position in a country to do that? You're throwing everything away [for a silly dream]!"

I'd love to pretend that those moments made me feel even more determined to prove them wrong, but they didn't.

I felt sad, a tad bit lonely, and very much misunderstood. I knew I had nothing to prove, but I also wanted them to experience what I had felt when I chose to align with the call. How could I even encourage their openness to Guidance when I had nothing to show for my openness yet?

I turned my focus to writing the book while closing off my obligations at my GM job over the next couple of months. I had this silly expectation that once I had listened to Guidance, I would be given superpowers, and the book would flow out of me like a modern-day genius.

And it did flow out of me — a lovely well of verbose, minus the genius.

Guidance Is God's Job. Structure Is Yours.

Does God only help those who help themselves? No. But does God need your help? Yes, in all acts of divine co-creation, you *need* to do your part.

I know there are a bunch of people squirming at such a concept — God, needing the help of us frail humans — but, I'm standing firmly by this until Future-Me learns more on the divine co-creation process.

My point is this: **you are the vessel through which these creations will pass. As such, the quality of the creation that's birthed into the world depends highly on the quality of your vessel. Your job is to ensure that this vessel is prepared to birth these creations, to the best of your current ability, and to get up tomorrow and do the same again.**

As a practical example, while I had followed Guidance to deep dive into the books, and even to become a publishing entrepreneur through my company, I had to put in a TONNE of work to ensure that the story of Yara would translate as best as it could to those who would become her readers.

As I confidently wrote the first five chapters (my sample size to ensure I was on the right track for engaging Yara's readers), I came face-to-face with an ego-smashing challenge. My boyfriend took on the role of my pseudo-developmental editor, and his truth is the brutal kind, oriented towards ensuring that you banish all chances of mediocrity. He read my first chapters, pointing out instances of me losing the thread or running away too quickly with the storyline or not catering to my reader's knowledge or trying to tell them what I could instead show them — you name it — and each time, I grumbled as my ego felt the burn… but I got to it and started again.

Finally, the day came when he told me that everything was okay, except the speed. I had rushed through the prose without taking the time to add in elements of the experience. My frustration grew to the point of explosion; then, I calmed down and reminded myself that these comments were only to my benefit. I sucked it up on a beautiful Sunday and sat down for six hours, without a single break, and edited the script line-by-line. I added in my adjectives and slowed my sentences, giving myself a chance to describe the beauty of all I could see through Yara's eyes.

When I had completed the rework, I passed it over to him, stuffed my face, and went to take a long, hot, satisfying bath. I couldn't even finish my bath without him interrupting, and as he entered the bathroom, I could only smile because I had been anticipating all that he would say.

Instead, he said: "Ummm… I don't like it. I prefer how it was before."

… Yeah… Ouch! He went on to explain that it felt like I had simply fluffed it up with adjectives and descriptions and now the script was dragging, and every other thing I *didn't* want to hear.

My ego had had enough. I ripped into him, saying that he wasn't an author or a "real" developmental editor, so clearly, he didn't know what he was doing. And he agreed, saying that this was the best he could do, and he wasn't going to be anything less than honest with me about how he felt in the reading experience.

I was determined to prove him wrong — so determined, in fact, that I began researching everything I could to send him ten million articles on how very, very wrong he was and how brilliant a writer I was. Instead, what I found were those same ten million articles telling me that he was one hundred percent right on every single thing he had perceived.

For those who enjoy the more technical nature of writing, my issue was my pacing. I hadn't mastered this whatsoever, so sometimes I sped, and other times I dragged while fluffing, both of which were cardinal sins to the script. Eventually, I found an incredible online course on pacing, learnt all about things like motivation-reaction units and how to string them together to help, and then I redid those first five chapters for (what felt like) the zillionth time.

And this time, when he read them, he smiled.

And Yes, Relationships Need Structure Too

Finally, I get to write a section in this book where *I was right*! [No, not about those five chapters, or becoming an author, but about building a metaphorical home/structure with the one you love.] Somebody! Anybody! Pop the champagne! Let's blow the roof off this house!

Okay, fine, I'm exaggerating — clearly — because the funny thing about life is that beyond the black-and-white basics, the notion of "right" is a fallacy. No matter what side of the coin you think you've landed on, each side will have the experience that facilitates what they need to learn individually and together.

For my Guidance-based relationship, although my approach to building that "house" with those "architectural plans" on our "common ground" had found its root in jaded intentions, the concept itself was a powerful one. Just like all acts of co-creation, the vessel needs to be the very best for the creation to also be the very best. And that takes structure, which is what my "house" had been aimed at creating.

The difference was that I had been trying to apply structure separate to tuning into Guidance. As for him, he defaulted more into only tuning into Guidance, rather than then applying a clear structure to funnel those new realities to which we were led. He wasn't wrong in what should come first — Guidance always has to come before structure for it to be an act of alignment. The other way around would become yet another lesson to learn the hard way. However, the structure was needed for this alignment to be empowered and effective.

When we opened ourselves to the other's side, we were able to combine our approaches into a powerful, divinely-driven system. We found a wealth of new depths which neither of us had ever dived before. Our lives became filled with signs and confirmations of the direction in which we should go next, and our ultimate job became to stay tuned in or to get back in tune. Any natural misunderstandings never lasted long, as we would both feel assured that we were where we were supposed to be — with each other — doing what we were supposed to do: following Guidance.

With this openness, "teachers" appeared through books and vlogs, and even through random movies and interactions. One of the "teachers" who appeared along this journey was none other than the brilliant — and at times, controversial — Dr Jordan Peterson. While his range of offerings is extensive, for the purposes of this writing, I'll focus exclusively in the section that follows on his Self-

Authoring Suite.

The True Test of Healing

How do you know, really know, if you're in the process of healing, or if you're finally there? Is it a lifelong pursuit? Can we ever really "arrive"? Is it when we return to how we were before the hurt? Is that possible, and should it be, if even the human body believes in keeping its scars?

I didn't quite know it at the time, but I had a sense that there was some work left to do. Still, you couldn't convince me that this work was mammoth-sized, because my life seemed to be on the up-and-up: I was in a steady, progressive, and hugely divine relationship; I had forgiven the man who had tried to take my life; I was listening to God's Guidance to the most seemingly ridiculous extent — I mean, I was writing storybooks now!

I moseyed along with my present, fully engaged and excited for the future, but I hadn't turned an eye towards processing where I had come from and all I had experienced. There were lessons there, gems really, but I was more than willing to forego those treasures and categorise them under "sunken ship; lost at war," rather than go diving to the darkest trench in my ocean to recover them.

Enter Dr Jordan Peterson and his Self-Authoring Suite which, according to the website (www.selfauthoring.com), was "a series of online writing programs that collectively help you explore your past, present and future." Dr Peterson's claim, as a clinical psychologist, was that "People who spend time writing carefully about themselves become happier, less anxious and depressed and physically healthier."

I remember my first exposure to this as being filled with intrigue. I loved journaling, and this seemed to be the perfect way to get a snapshot of my life (where I was at) and to affirm where I'd want to be. It felt like the reset I needed, offered through a brilliantly-devised structure that I could only liken to self-therapy. The Suite had such powerful results from its programmes that, despite being someone who cringed at the thought of ever talking to a therapist, I was fascinated.

I decided that this would be the perfect gift to give myself, and with one reasonable online "swipe," I started my self-authoring journey. I jumped into the Future Authoring immediately, eyes set on what would come should I fulfil all of my dreams. The questions went deep, helping me to sort through the person I wanted to be, all the way down to the obstacles and their solutions, my motives/intentions, and how I would monitor my progress. However, as I worked through it, I kept eyeing the Past Authoring, feeling a slight distaste.

To distract and perhaps convince myself that this wouldn't be a problem, I jumped into the Present Authoring section on Faults. I wanted to prove how happy and able I was to accept my weaknesses, and feel my willingness to work on them. I eyed the Past again; my distaste grew. To combat it, I read the details surrounding the Past Authoring in an attempt to dispel the narrative I was telling myself.

The website claimed, "It would be particularly useful to complete the Past Authoring Program if you have memories that are more than about eighteen months old that still intrude upon your thoughts, or that still evoke emotion such as fear, regret, shame or confusion. If this is happening, it means that your mind has not yet been able to process your past experiences fully and that the brain areas associated with negative emotion still regard the past events in question as unresolved threats. This is not good, because your brain reacts to unresolved threats with emergency physiological preparation, including the production of stress hormones such as cortisol that can be very toxic when chronically elevated."

And so, in realising how much shame, confusion, fear, and regret I felt about so many areas in my past, I closed off the website and never returned. [Run, Jeanelle, run]

Yeah, You Can Dip In The Water — But You'll Still Drown

You can run, but you can't hide. I mean, it hasn't been more than a couple of years since I closed that website page and here I am, writing an entire exposé of my past for the world to read. However, let's not jump ahead without me first telling you how I got here.

Three months after I handed in my resignation, I released the first book of The YaraStar Trilogy, called The Unmarked Girl. I wailed like a baby, both for the terror of people having access to my imaginary world, and the intense road I had taken to get there. The timeline was a form of madness too, but I wanted to enter my new year of life finally *being* who I had sensed within myself. Whatever price I paid, including the little errors scantly littered throughout the prose, was more than worth it!

While I will leave the plot unsoiled for those who

wish to venture into its pages, in writing book one into book two, I soon realised that *God* had once again set me up. Elements of my past battles began to spill themselves all over the pages through analogies and metaphors in Yara's more detailed journey. She battled my battles, fought my wars, made stupid decisions like me, and found herself in some of the most disconcerting situations on her planet. And it wasn't just her character that did this. Every single side character represented another side of me and my story, in ways that brought me to my knees.

Essentially, I was writing a massive analogy of Dr Peterson's Past-Authoring — the opposite of what I had wanted! Before I could back out, I had already committed to putting myself through this insane torture three times in a row. Each book held a K.O. [knock out] like no other, and the more I buckled, the more I knew that I was not being allowed to run from this.

This was the climb. And this was the reason: **I cannot fully embrace all of who I am, and am to become, without first facing, with love and forgiveness, all of who I've been.** My vessel needed to be readied for the road ahead, and no matter where I had tried to run, I always, always, ended up back in my past. It became undeniable: my progress away from my past depended on my ability to process it, as well as my choice to trust that process.

The Point Of Trust

I gave in, to all of it, through Yara. I began to come to terms with the parts of myself I couldn't understand or didn't want to accept, and I soon welcomed my darker sides, along with my commitment to light. My denial had cost me so much, as had my running and screaming and fearing the entirety of, well, me.

Each book of the trilogy followed a theme that I had followed throughout the process of writing them:

1. Finding myself
2. Knowing myself
3. Being myself

As my walls gently lowered with each lesson contained in those themes, I found my soul becoming lighter and more open to the flow of life. My stress levels began to lower, and my outlook grew brighter. I giggled more when I saw confirmations and signs along my journey, feeling the kind of thrill I had only felt when I was a child.

In all of this, a powerful anchor appeared: **no matter what was happening, even if it was horrible at the moment, I only needed to trust that I was being led to and through it for a divine reason.** With that anchor, even if I momentarily lost sight of it, I could return to a place of inexplicable peace. I knew solutions would present themselves with just the right timing, and that even if I veered off course, I could return to the path in an instant by simply tuning in.

The more I trusted in my divine path even through the storms, the more I found myself in the eye of them, aware that they existed all around me, but unaffected in the most profound of ways. I only ever needed to trust the process, the unfolding of life, while giving my all to crafting the best possible vessel out of myself, and *God* would reveal the next step.

If you've ever done any formal dancing with a partner, you'll know that One takes the lead and the other allows themselves to be led. As the one being led, this dance didn't require me to know what was coming next for me to flow with my Partner *gracefully*. I only needed to engage with openness, fluidity, and flexibility for this co-creation to shine.

It doesn't matter if you see God in a religious way or a spiritual way or in multiple forms or with a different name, but I do have a question:

Do you know, or want to know, what it feels like to dance with *God*?

CHAPTER NINE

THE PEAK OF WORSHIP

As your hand grasped the top of the steepest ledge you'd ever scaled, a surge of exhilarating energy powered through your being. A smile broke out on your face when you put an extra leap into your final pull, hoisting your body up and over onto the top of the edge of your mountain. This was it; this was the moment it had all been for, right here, right now.

As you stood up straight and surveyed the breathtaking beauty that surrounded you, tears came to your eyes. The trees stood strong, and they relished the warmth of the evening's sun. Many were laden with fruits you'd never seen before, and as the birds pecked and fluttered, you laughed at their delight. The scent of spring water filled your nose, and the gurgling sounds of its nearby source refreshed your senses.

This mountain was a jewel unlike anything you could have imagined, but as the sun began to set, you knew you'd underestimated the rarity of its existence. All around you, the blades of grass and trunks of trees and creatures of water and land picked up a growing glow against the darkening sky. Each one combated the darkness by producing their bioluminescent light as it bled off their surfaces with soft glimmers. Sparkling wonderment would fill even the darkest nights on your mountains; you could not believe that this was your home.

When you'd had your fill of every crevice you could find, you peered back off the ledge and towards the valley from which you had come, but, feeling a sense of sadness, you looked away.

The next morning when you awoke, however, you heard not one but two songs on the wind, and you walked back to the ledge to hear them. One you recognised, and you could only huff and then laugh as the Valley teased:

"I was made for the weak so that they could become strong. How does it feel to know your true strength, dear traveller?"

You gazed upon the shrouded valley, hidden in the shadows of the trees and the midst of the fog, and allowed yourself to feel. You let the wind carry your thoughts back into memories and your heart back into a life gone past. As you did, the fogs began to clear, and the path you had taken was ignited by inexplicable lights that shone with pride. You felt a little embarrassed, seeing the many times you'd gone in a different direction and the laps you'd made around the same point, but that feeling soon dissipated in both the hilarity and existentialism of it all. Each point resounded with a place at which you'd grown, and at that moment, you knew it had all been for a great purpose. None of your pain had been in vain. If you had not grown so strong, you could never have scaled the near-vertical rock face of the steepest mountain.

Still, it was the second song — the one you didn't recognise — that pulled your attention now. It said one thing, and one thing only:

"There is always love for you here."

You tried to detect where it was coming from, but it seemed to be so far away. Soon, though, your eyes caught a glimpse through the still-parting fog, and you followed its unfolding billows all the way to —

"My birth mountain…"

It had been ages since you'd allowed yourself to remember it, and much longer since you'd seen it, yet as it appeared through the mist, you recognised its glorious form. As the memories of your early years crept back in, a warmth entered with them, and the softest of smiles. Your birth mountain had taught you so much about the innocence of life, and the duality that comes from belonging in two places, until you found the secret to navigating your path: belonging only to your calling.

Then, as if a little girl once again, you remembered the sheer thrill of climbing the highest trees at the highest points of the mountain, and you turned and ran. You leapt over streams and swung through trees and climbed up rocks, higher and higher, until you saw the tree that stood at the very top of your mountain.

Then, you slowed your pace and savoured every step you made towards it. With your right foot, you gave thanks that you finally knew the way you were meant to live in alignment, and with your left foot, you gave thanks for all of life's curveballs that had realigned you when you lost your way.

Upon reaching the tree, you gripped the first branch with your right hand and gave thanks for the foundation your birth mountain had given. When you gripped with your left, you gave thanks for the destined mountain upon which you would build your new home.

Step by step, grip by grip, you ascended to the very tippy-top of the tallest tree on the mountain of your becoming, and it was there that you breathed in all that your life had once been, now was, and would become. As a shower of glimpses from your unfolding destiny, more powerful than ever before, rained upon you with all of its blessings, you breathed out the words that could only be described as worship:

"I'm here; I'm finally home. And I'm ready."

Why "Worship"

When I first asked for the name of this book, the word "worship" was the only thing I was shown that should be included. Whatever words surrounded it were my structure to give, but I was not to compromise, under any circumstances, on the use of that word in the title.

I groaned as I typed what I'd been given into my journal, and then I closed it and returned to my life. There was no way, after all of my battles with religion and spirituality, that *God* was going to make **me**, *of all the people in the world*, write a book with that word anywhere near the name [yet, here we are, so guess who chose *not* to learn her lesson the hard way… well, this time].

You know what? Let's up the ante here: I was not even totally okay with using the word "God" because of how many limits I've felt like religion places on its use. Over time, my inner battles have been extensive, covering everything from the existence of God to the human representation of God on the Earth. I longed for the seeming surety the afterlife promised — the answers to my many existential questions.

In my youth, during those dogmatic Christian days, I might have driven more people away from God than towards (I'll leave this up for debate). I was out there raining fire and judgement on anyone who dared to utter an approach that varied from my convictions. Even with my hidden questions, I still believed I was doing right by God, while likely being the very best example of the reason many ran away. That should have been a litmus test I used — testing whether my words and life brought people closer to or further away from God — to know if I was the light I claimed (WWJD-style).

After this period, I didn't want to be associated with the person I once was. Since then, even when meaning "God," I preferred to use terms like "Divinity," and I even tried on the good ole "Universe" for size (no, not so I could worship an idol called "The Universe," but because I felt so far removed from the portrayal of "God" from my past). Words carry so much meaning and, through this discomfort, I realised that they can even be a trigger for trauma.

But, I digress.

Ultimately, more so for those of us who aren't atheists, there is an ever-present part of us that acknowledges the presence of Someone (Something?) with the divine master-plan, always beyond human comprehension. This is who I've referred to in the context of my entire book. The *God* I believe in is not limited to the words any human language chooses to assign. God, it turns out, is also not limited by the extent of my past trauma.

Now, when I reach out to ask for God's Guidance, this is and always will be a private communication — between God and me — outside the scope of any human's ability or position to know, judge, or understand.

Yet, despite eventually understanding this, I felt pure trepidation claiming that word in such a powerful way while writing this book. Was it that I felt undeserving of such a sacred form of communion with God? Maybe. Did I allow that fear, unworthiness, and shame to conquer me? By evidence of what you're reading, no.

But what made writing this book, with God all up in here, so crucial?

Well, it's because we humans have allowed everyone and everything other than *God* to dictate what is hot, cold, and lukewarm for us. As a result, many have defaulted to separating spirituality from their daily living. This may be because, like me, they were told that the ways they connected to Divinity weren't "right" or "acceptable" to God. They may have been given ultimatums for how to approach this all-encompassing sacredness, with the consequence of being excommunicated or persecuted or chastised by all manner of people. If those presented with these ultimatums felt like the religiously "right" way didn't resonate with them, they were far more likely to put aside all spiritual pursuits. They may have settled into a life devoid of what I believe is **the most powerful anchor we should have: a spiritual one.**

I'm *not* okay with this. It bothers me to my core, so much so that I had to get to the root of my why. Was it because of all I had experienced? Certainly — but, everything we've been through serves our journey and purpose.

In exploring my why, I discovered that I had no issue with, and only admiration for, those who fully committed to living the ways they believed were right for their lives. The issue only arose when those who made this commitment also needed everyone else to be wrong for them to be right. It was likely because, in their beliefs, anyone else also being right meant they would be wrong, and their defences would come crashing down. Thus, many of them seemed to see this "rightness" as an entitlement reserved only for their paths, and having been one of "them" in my early years, I understand that.

Somewhere along the way, we all lost sight of the most critical aspect in this: if God is as powerful as we believe, then anyone who is sincerely reaching out to Him/Her will most certainly find that divine, destined connection. What matters, above all else, is that humans access that connection by opening their hearts to reach out. In times like these, a spiritual anchor is what we need. All we need to do is ask for that divine Guidance on how we are to live, and then listen. God can let *each of us* know the rest. For me, to be "hot" is to surrender to God's will.

Thus, worship, in my "modern" way of viewing it, was not limited to religious services or even defined/approved ways in which it should take place to be considered worship. It wasn't *only* found in a pause in the day to pray, or a genre of music or even a song (though there are many I love —

especially from Hillsong). It could also be present in the way I made my coffee or how I exercised, the way I typed up an email or hugged a friend, the path to valuing my sensuality or the way I loved the love of my life. It could even be accessed in the offices of politicians or the most dangerous parts of the ghettos: *anyone* could find that spiritual anchor and then choose to surrender to God's will for *every choice* in thought, word, and deed.

Worship was *not* reserved for those who claimed to be religious or the "right denomination." No one was entitled above anyone else to this sacred communion with God. Worship belonged, and has always belonged, to all of the people on this planet through their connection to God. It was accessible not just in seemingly direct ways of reaching out, but also in the smallest, most insignificant actions.

Why? Because worship is a way of living. To that end, I believe that anyone, anywhere, can connect the details of their lives to the unique master-plan that's designed for them. To me, this is the highest connection you can make with God: worship.

However, you've got to trust that you're more than capable of having that connection without needing the validation of any person on this planet.

Inner Authority VS Outer Authority

I want to be even more open. Wait, is that possible after all we've covered thus far? I feel like my soul is already on a platter in front of you right now, so let me jump right into another one of my potentially controversial beliefs:

I believe God can use anyone, or anything, to deliver messages to you.

I've received such directions through everything and anything, from the Bible to other religious texts, to strangers and friends, and even to horoscopes I scrolled past on Instagram, and scenes or lines in Netflix shows. The way I differentiate between what has divine meaning for me or a situation unfolding in my life, versus what doesn't, is the peace-inducing nudge I feel within me when it happens.

There is a connectedness that transpires when you choose to live your life in surrender to your calling. You receive access to a matrix of infinite touchpoints that can lead you in a variety of directions along the path to which you're called. A dog's bark can sound like the rhythm for a song, the tagline of an advertisement may provide the missing piece of a puzzle, and the various spiritual concepts throughout the world can broaden your radar's perspective.

One such experience I had was when I was beginning to understand a relatively new but complex belief system called Human Design. While I'll leave the details of this for the professionals in the field, there were two concepts called "Inner Authority" and "Outer Authority" that I found fascinating.

From what I understood, we humans tend to use our rational minds to make decisions for our lives. This is called "outer authority," and it isn't just present in our discussions with ourselves, but also with others. Whenever we seek the advice of others to lead us (rather than accepting it as mere potential wisdom), we are not aligned with our designs. We should only make decisions when we are tuned in to ourselves (inner authority). Thus, only inner authority can tell us whether a decision is correct for us or not. Learning this, I likened the inner authority to God's will.

In the very way my parents exposed me to the crucial need to have a spiritual anchor, which in turn helped me to be open when I finally decided to find *my* unique anchor, so too can outer authority help on the journey to finding inner authority.

For this reason, I want to hinge every single thing I've shared, whether in this book or otherwise, on this exact concept. I want you to know that if anything here doesn't resonate with you, then follow your Guidance on it. Discard what doesn't align with who you're here to be, even if you have to throw this entire book in the trash!

This world needs people who are willing to believe wholly and fully in the sacred nudges they feel within themselves. It needs humans who will follow their callings through valleys and up mountains and in deserts — wherever, however, and whenever they hear that call.

It is why I know my parents are supposed to be the incredible and evolved Christians they are today, even if our practised beliefs may differ, and it's even why I knew I was meant to write Yara's trilogy.

Yara Becomes a Star

Less than a year after the first book of The YaraStar Trilogy (The Unmarked Girl) was released, this book won a regional award called the CODE Burt Award for Caribbean Young Adult Literature (2019). That same year, the book received a Kirkus Star [from Kirkus Reviews: a highly esteemed American book review magazine], made Kirkus Reviews'

Best 100 Indie Books of 2019 List, and was also listed in their five Best Indie Middle-Grade & YA Books of 2019.

I'm sharing this not because every step we take in alignment will be so discernibly rewarded — sometimes, the reward is to be aligned — but because I want you to know that you are always being sent in exactly the direction you're supposed to walk when you surrender to God's will. As such, my favourite line from Guidestar (an ethereal character in the trilogy) comes from that place:

"Your power is in your surrender."

Years before this, the word "surrender" seemed like a choice for the weak and the defeated. For those who no longer had a fight left in them, who gave in to the pressures of life and others, who would even bow to religion or politics or money — shameful surrender would be their path. But for me, the brave, strong, ego-driven me, you would never get me to submit, ever!

I was a relentless soul, even if it had almost cost me my life. I didn't believe in giving in or giving up. It took me a long time, through the dark ages of my soul, to realise that the only thing I needed to be unrelenting in was the act of surrender.

It became a superpower of its own. Any time I felt

the doubt, fear, frustration, shame, regret, and anger trying to conquer my resolve, I would ask myself, "Am I following God's will? Have I submitted to Guidance?"

And once I knew I was, I would surrender all that stood in the way of my trust, peace, love, and joy. Even in the face of darkness and uncertainty and destruction, even if they had all been caused by some new crappy mistake I'd made, I found myself right back at that altar to realign, surrender, and go again.

What If You're Wrong?

Let's say that one day, you misinterpreted or made a move without that Guidance. Basically, you led yourself down the "wrong" path, despite convincing yourself it was the "right" one, and this caused seeds of doubt and insecurity to take root within you. How could you ever trust yourself again?

Hey! Tell me any doubt you've had: I've thought it, felt it, but eventually, I've conquered it.

How? Well, after a while, I realised that I needed to be okay with feeling like I'd got it "wrong" sometimes. We're humans! We're flawed! Take a deep breath! It's okay! This isn't a quest for perfection. I mean, have you read my story?! If it were about that, a large part of my life has been a failure, and I might as well be dead.

There is a mastery that only comes when we practice tuning in, and even then, we will still make mistakes. If you're looking for a "destination" to aim for, mastery — not perfection — is as good as it gets.

Let yourself be "wrong." Then, remind yourself that, technically, there's no such thing. There are only lessons which you can use to either lift yourself up or put yourself down, and one of the most powerful things you can do to lift yourself up is to own your story.

Owning My Story

This brings us here, as I type these words to you, in the final pages of having owned my story. It isn't as comprehensive as an early autobiography, and nor does it spell out every mistake or triumph or ellipsis in between. Instead, it seeks to examine my spiritual journey through a very real and raw lens in the hopes that it may encourage you to explore yours.

When I decided to face my past fully, in many ways,

it brought me to my knees. I found myself steeped in the pain and shame of who I once was. I felt consumed by anger against Past-Me, almost like she had betrayed the person she knew I wanted to become. She left me with a lot of mess to clean up, and I mean *a lot*. I didn't feel like I had what it took to clear out *her* mess from under the sky-high rug.

Thankfully, there is a vulnerability that comes from love, and there is no greater vulnerability you can experience than loving your messiest parts. It doesn't mean you have to share them with the world — not unless you're so led — but it does mean you have to face them as your most naked self.

To be naked in this regard is to be honest with yourself when you feel ashamed or angry or hurt by what you did or who you were, and then get to the deepest why of each of those emotions. Dr Peterson's Self-Authoring Suite is a tool I highly recommend, despite my initial panic-based scamper from its show-and-tell-it-all mirror. There, or in whatever method you choose, you can give Past-You compassion for not only what it is to be human, but also what it is to be dark, hurt, and hurtful, or even violent and terrifying. We talk so much about forgiving ourselves because "we didn't know better," but there are so many people out there — myself included — who felt at points that they *did* know better, and they hate themselves for their self-inflicted betrayal.

They may even be facing consequences that have cost them their health (mental and physical), the people they love, and even their very freedom because of their past choices and the laws that govern our world. To have a constant reminder of who you used to be hanging over your head even while you try to become the person you know you could be is a tremendous burden. I want you to take heart. If this speaks to you, know that your journey (even its worst parts) is uniquely intertwined with your purpose. Wherever you are, whatever the circumstances, your purpose is always, *always*, right there with you.

To own your story is cathartic in ways I wish I could put you into my soul to feel. Your soul deserves to be cleansed. You deserve to feel the lightness of processed pain and inexplicable trust, no matter what storms are brewing. You deserve to catch glimpses of your destiny and to allow them to fuel your days with the passion of purpose.

And you deserve the harvest that pain can produce through living a life of worship.

The Final Catch

I questioned whether to include this part, as I'd hate to discourage anyone at the start of their journey (those readying themselves to leave their birth mountains). Even those in their valley experiences may curse under their breaths when I share this little (BIG) plot twist. However, the most I can tell you is my truth, and by now, I hope you know to follow your Guidance far above the words in this book or any other.

So, here's the catch: once you've journeyed from your birth mountain through the dark valley of your soul to find, and ascend, your peak, another mountain may one day send its song on the winds to you.

Some are given the exceptional 'luck' of making only one journey, and they spend their lives ascending their mountains, or perhaps going back down to the valley to encourage others along their paths.

However, there will be those among you who, having faced and conquered these skeletons and demons and monsters, will then be asked to journey through a new valley to do it all over again. It may be that your mountain was a career track or a marriage or a country or even a belief system. You'd learnt all you were meant to there, and you were asked to move on to another path beyond your range of experience.

It may be disconcerting and it may be horrifying, but if you've allowed yourself to learn the lessons of the journey, and you've practised what it means to tune into your Guidance, then it doesn't have to be the terror you might have experienced the first time around.

You can move within the eye of the storm *indefinitely*, but you have to move with God. If you end up in the storm itself, you have to find your way back to that place of inner peace and trust, and then keep moving.

The Peak Of Worship

I look back upon my journey thus far with nothing but warmth and peace flooding my being. There were so many points along the way that I didn't understand until I ascended my new mountain and gained insight through its retrospective view; I know now that all was as it should have been.

I'm still climbing and exploring this mountain. There's much to discover here, but my very best moments upon it remain when I am at the peak of worship: aligning myself with God's will.

What is worship for you? I'd love to know all the ways it shows up in your life's journey. Here's just one of mine:

I've started singing again.

P.S. Maybe one day I'll share some of my music. Perhaps I've already been guided to do so. Still, here's someone else's perfect song for our parting moment: ***Sia – Bird Set Free***

THE END

…AND, ALWAYS, A NEW BEGINNING.

RECAP THE JOURNEY

As a reminder of the journey, I'm going to bring all of our points together here. For some points, you may have learnt enough to skip them — count yourself as blessed! Or, there may be points unique to you that I haven't included here as you're even more of an overachiever than I was at learning lessons the hard way. No matter what, this is your journey, your inimitable, horrifying, beautiful, enthralling, mysterious path to your purpose, with every step drowned in precisely that: purpose.

1. **The Point Of Origin:** your birth mountain, or current mountain, upon which your foundation has been built.
2. **The Point Of First Awakening:** your duality, usually fuelled by the appearance of the calling of Guidance towards a new or different way of being.
3. **The Point Of No Return:** your actioned commitment to follow the call, even if you're ill-prepared and unsupported. You enter the valley here.
4. **The Point Of Brokenness:** your rock-bottom that tends to occur when you continually numb out or silence your Guidance instead of trusting the call.

5. **The Point Of Turning:** your recognition that your current approach isn't one of alignment, and your steps towards changing it.
6. **The Point Of Renewal:** your renewed connection to the call of Guidance and the re-commitment you make to follow it no matter where it leads.
7. **The Point Of Alignment:** your period of divine testing begins to ensure your steps are steady as you make your way to the mountain that is yours to climb. You find your divine mountain here.
8. **The Point Of Trust:** your climb begins, strengthened through the valley journey and the tests you've passed in following the call. Your steps are strong and guided.
9. **The Peak Of Worship:** as you remain in the centre of God's will, with a daily commitment, you actualise all you were placed on the planet to be.

RESOURCES

This isn't an exhaustive resource list, but I found these websites to be helpful. I hope they help you too.

Learn about Dr Jordan Peterson's Self-Authoring Suite here: https://www.selfauthoring.com/

Learn more about violence against women here:
https://www.who.int/news-room/fact-sheets/detail/violence-against-women

Learn about the Signs of a Domestic Abuser here:
http://www.hiddenhurt.co.uk/warning_signs.html

Find Help for Abusers here:
http://www.hiddenhurt.co.uk/help_for_abusers.html

Learn about Sexual Consent here:
https://www.plannedparenthood.org/learn/relationships/sexual-consent

ACKNOWLEDGEMENTS

Kevin: You never bat an eyelid when I tell you the next crazy thing I'm guided to do, yet you're always batting for me, in my corner in every possible way. Thank you for being my love, my family, my best friend, my business partner, and my forever-aligned. I love you!

Mum & Dad: I know that there may be many things within these pages that evoke thoughts and feelings beyond my capacity to comfort or change. Still, to know that our family's love is unconditional, just as God's is, will forever be a blessing. I love you both!

Alyxander the Great: You witnessed the writing of this book, from start to finish, and you celebrated its content and completion as though it were your own (even if you may need to be a bit older to read it). We all got to celebrate you as well, my brilliant boy, as you excelled in all of your studies despite the crazy COVID-19 year. What did I do to deserve such an incredible twelve-year-old son? Gosh… I love you — by infinity!

ABOUT THE AUTHOR

JEANELLE FRONTIN

"The one thing I'm not is one thing."

Simple as it may be, Jeanelle's adage has been a consistent reminder of her limitless freedom to choose "all of the above" when exploring varied passions. As a result, she has never been afraid of having a diverse lifestyle. Actively involved in various fields, from engineering to the creative industries, she's the co-founder of Mark Made Group Ltd.: a creative company focused on enabling adept humans and choice projects to make their mark on the world. She was born in the Caribbean, in Trinidad and Tobago, and she firmly believes that every human being on this planet should experience her native islands. Honoured to be the mother of Alyxander, the son of her greatest dreams, she dedicates her work to him.

www.jeanellefrontin.com

Find me @jeanellefrontin everywhere!

Printed in Great Britain
by Amazon

61760229R00150